WHAT EVERYONE NEEDS TO KNOW ABOUT THE Holy Spirit

DON STEWART

What Everyone Needs to Know about the Holy Spirit
Who Is the Spirit of God?

© 2017 by Don Stewart

Published by EOW (Educating Our World)
www.educatingourworld.com
All rights reserved

English Versions Cited
The various English versions which we cite in this course, apart from the King James Version, all have copyrights. They are listed as follows.

Verses marked NIV are taken from the HOLY BIBLE, New International Version 2011, Copyright 1973 1978, 1984, 2011 by International Bible Society. Used by permission of Zondervan Publishing House. All rights reserved.

Scripture quotations marked CSB have been taken from the Christian Standard Bible®, Copyright © 2017 by Holman Bible Publishers.

Verses marked ESV are from The Holy Bible English Standard Version™ Copyright © 2001 by Crossway Bibles, a division of Good News Publishers All rights reserved.

Scripture quotations marked (NLT) are taken from the Holy Bible, New Living Translation, copyright 1996. Used by permission of Tyndale House Publishers, Inc., Wheaton, Illinois 60189. All rights reserved.

Scripture quotations marked "NKJV" are taken from the New King James Version. Copyright © 1982 by Thomas Nelson, Inc. All rights reserved. Used by permission.

Scripture quotations marked CEV are taken from the Contemporary English Version (CEV) copyright American Bible Society 1991, 1995

Scripture quoted by permission. Quotations designated NET are from the NET Bible Copyright © 2003 By Biblical Studies Press, L.L.C. www.netbible.com All rights reserved.

GOD'S WORD is a copyrighted work of God's Word to the Nations. Quotations are used by permission. Copyright 1995 by God's Word to the Nations. All rights reserved.

TABLE OF CONTENTS

QUESTION 1: WHY IS IT IMPORTATN TO STUDY THE SUBJECT OF THE HOLY SPIRIT 7

QUESTION 2: What Is the Proper Way to Approach the Subject of the Spirit of God? 15

QUESTION 3: Why Is the Subject of the Holy Spirit Neglected? 19

QUESTION 4: Who Is the Holy Spirit? (The Spirit of God) 25

QUESTION 5: Is the Holy Spirit a Person? 29

QUESTION 6: Does the New Testament Depart from the Normal Rules of Grammar to Indicate the Personhood of the Holy Spirit? 51

QUESTION 7: Could the Holy Spirit Merely Be the Personification of God's Power? 55

QUESTION 8: Why Is the Holy Spirit Spoken of in the Neuter Gender? 65

QUESTION 9: Why Do Some Argue That the Holy Spirit Is an Impersonal Force? 69

QUESTION 10: What Do We Learn about the Nature of the Spirit of God from the Old Testament? 75

QUESTION 11: Is the Holy Spirit Called God? 79

QUESTION 12: Is the Holy Spirit Associated on an Equal Basis with God the Father and God the Son? 85

QUESTION 13: Does the Holy Spirit Have the Attributes of God? 89

QUESTION 14: Has the Holy Spirit Performed Divine Works? 97

QUESTION 15: What Different Titles are Ascribed to the Spirit of God? 109

QUESTION 16: Should the Holy Spirit Be Singled out for Worship? 121

QUESTION 17: Whom Does the Holy Spirit Proceed From? (Procession, *Filioque* Controversy) 125

QUESTION 18: What Is the "Name" of the Holy Spirit? 131

QUESTION 19: Who Are the Seven Spirits? 135

QUESTION 20: Is There a Counterfeit Holy Spirit? 141

QUESTION 21: What Symbols Does the Bible Use to Describe the Holy Spirit? 145

QUESTION 22: Why Is the Holy Spirit Compared to a Dove? 151

QUESTION 23: Why Is the Holy Spirit Compared to Water? 159

QUESTION 24: Why Is the Holy Spirit Compared to Fire? 165

QUESTION 25: Why Is the Holy Spirit Compared to the Wind? 169

QUESTION 26: Why Is the Holy Spirit Compared to Clothing? 175

QUESTION 27: Why Is the Holy Spirit Compared to a Pledge or Guarantee? 179

QUESTION 28: Why Is the Holy Spirit Associated with the Anointing of Oil? 183

QUESTION 29: Why Is the Seal, or Insignia, a Symbol of God's Spirit? 189

QUESTION 30: Is There a Difference between the Holy Spirit and the Holy Ghost? 193

ABOUT THE AUTHOR 197

Introduction

There are certain things which everyone should know about the Holy Spirit. In this book, we will find out what the Bible specifically has to say about the Spirit of God.

Who is the Holy Spirit? Is He merely a force that comes from God, or is He more than that?

We will discover that the biblical teaching on the Holy Spirit is clear—He is a Person, a Divine Person. Indeed, the Holy Spirit is God—the Third Person of the Holy Trinity. As we shall see, Scripture makes this abundantly clear.

This volume is actually the first of a seven-book series on the subject of the Holy Spirit. Other volumes will explore such topics as: how the Spirit of God works, the various gifts of the Holy Spirit, whether all the gifts still exist today, speaking in tongues, the baptism with the Holy Spirit, and divine healing.

We trust that this series will not only clear up a number of common misconceptions about the Spirit of God, but that it will also add to the reader a greater knowledge and understanding of Him.

QUESTION 1

Why Is It Important to Study the Subject of the Holy Spirit?

The doctrine of the Holy Spirit is one of the most important subjects that a human being can study—if one wishes to know the major teachings of the Christian faith. Indeed, it is a significant subject of study for the following reasons:

1. THERE IS RENEWED INTEREST IN THE SUBJECT BY BELIEVERS

Until recently, believers have generally neglected the study of the Holy Spirit. However, in modern times there has been a tremendous interest in His Person and work. Today, like never before, believers are talking about the Holy Spirit.

However, with all the interest in the subject of the Spirit of God, there have been a variety of different opinions concerning who the Holy Spirit is, as well as how He works. This has led to confusion on the part of a number of believers. This makes it crucial to do a thorough biblical study on the subject.

2. THERE IS STILL TOO MUCH IGNORANCE OF THE SUBJECT

Unfortunately, there is still a great deal of ignorance with respect to the Person and work of the Holy Spirit. Many sincere Christians know little or nothing about Him. This ignorance has a number of practical implications.

For example, if we conceive of the Holy Spirit as an impersonal force, or some mere influence, then we will attempt to discover how we can use Him.

However, if we understand that the Holy Spirit is actually a divine Person, then our desire will be to discover how He can use us! This makes a detailed study of the subject of God's Spirit as something that is very important.

3. BELIEF ABOUT THE HOLY SPIRIT HAS CAUSED DIVISION AMONG CHRISTIANS

While Bible-believing Christians generally agree about the Person of God the Father, and the Person of God the Son, Jesus Christ, there is much division concerning the Holy Spirit and certain aspects of His work.

Unhappily, there are some people who believe that they, themselves, belong to a superior order of Christians because of their unique relationship with the Holy Spirit. As we will see, this type of arrogant attitude is the complete opposite of how the Spirit of God works in an individual.

In addition, opinions also vary as to the meaning and purpose of spiritual gifts. In fact, many churches have split over differing views of the Holy Spirit. This makes it important to have a proper biblical view of what the Holy Spirit does and what He does not do.

4. THERE IS FALSE DOCTRINE SURROUNDING THE PERSON OF THE HOLY SPIRIT

There is much false doctrine that is taught with respect to the identity of the Holy Spirit. In fact, many false teachers deny the personality and Deity of the Holy Spirit.

However, the Holy Spirit is not an "it" or some impersonal "thing." Indeed, He is God, Himself. Therefore, a complete, biblical picture of the Holy Spirit needs to be developed so this doctrine will not be distorted or denied.

5. THE SUBJECT OF THE HOLY SPIRIT IS PART OF BIBLE DOCTRINE

The doctrine of the Holy Spirit is contained in Holy Scripture. Furthermore, believers are commanded to study the entire counsel of God's Word because all of it is beneficial. The Apostle Paul wrote to Timothy:

> All Scripture is God-breathed and is useful for teaching, rebuking, correcting and training in righteousness (2 Timothy 3:16 NIV).

The fact that all Scripture is God-breathed, and the subject of the Holy Spirit is contained in Scripture, gives us another reason to devote time to studying this important topic.

Paul also wrote to Timothy:

> Work hard so God can approve you. Be a good worker, one who does not need to be ashamed and who correctly explains the word of truth (2 Timothy 2:15 NLT).

Therefore, a study of the Person and work of the Holy Spirit is vital.

6. THERE IS A LARGE AMOUNT OF SPACE IN SCRIPTURE DEVOTED TO THE SUBJECT

Not only is the doctrine of the Holy Spirit taught in Scripture, a tremendous amount of space is devoted to this subject. From Genesis to Revelation, from the creation of the world to the new heavens and new earth, the Holy Spirit is seen at work in our world. In fact, the Holy Spirit is mentioned some 90 times in the Old Testament with at least 18 different titles assigned to Him.

He is also mentioned more than 260 times in the New Testament. Only two of the 27 books of the New Testament, 2 John and 3 John, do not mention the Holy Spirit.

Each of the four gospels records that at the beginning of Jesus' ministry the outpouring of the Holy Spirit was promised. Hence, it is important for us to know as much as possible about who the Holy Spirit is, as well as what He does.

7. IT IS A DOCTRINE THAT IS UNIQUE TO THE CHRISTIAN FAITH

The doctrine of the Holy Spirit is unique to the Christian faith. There is no other religion that has a similar belief as this. Therefore, there is no comparison with any other religious system and no other frame of reference. Scripture, alone, must be the guide.

8. THE HOLY SPIRIT IS GOD

The Holy Spirit is God Almighty—the Third Person of the Holy Trinity. For this reason alone, the study of the Person and work of the Holy Spirit ought to be a priority when examining the Christian faith. If someone wants to know about the true God, then they need to know about the Holy Spirit.

9. THE HOLY SPIRIT RESIDES INSIDE BELIEVERS

Since the Holy Spirit is the one member of the Trinity that lives inside each believer, it is imperative that we know as much about Him as we can. From a practical standpoint, the understanding of how the Holy Spirit works can better equip believers to serve the Lord.

If we wrongly think of the Holy Spirit as some impersonal power, then we will attempt to find out how to get more of that power. However, if we see the Holy Spirit the way the Bible portrays Him, as God Himself, then we will attempt to find out how the Holy Spirit can get more of us.

10. THE HOLY SPIRIT IS THE UNIFIER OF BELIEVERS

The Holy Spirit is the one member of the Holy Trinity that unifies the body of Christ. The Apostle Paul wrote:

Make every effort to keep the unity of the Spirit through the bond of peace. There is one body and one Spirit, just as you were called to one hope when you were called; one Lord, one faith, one baptism; one God and Father of all, who is over all and through all and in all (Ephesians 4:3-6 NIV).

Since unity among believers is something to be desired, it is crucial to know about the One who preserves that unity. Hopefully, a study of the Holy Spirit will help unify believers.

11. THE DOCTRINE OF THE HOLY SPIRIT IS IMPORTANT FOR WORSHIP

Since the Holy Spirit is God, He is worthy to receive our adoration and worship. Thus, it is important to understand the God we are worshipping. This can only occur by means of diligent study of this Third Person of the Trinity.

12. THE DOCTRINE IS IMPORTANT FOR A BALANCED CHRISTIAN LIFE

The study of the various workings of the Holy Spirit is not a mere academic exercise. Indeed, it is something that is immensely practical and personal. The proper conception of the Holy Spirit allows the believer to live a balanced Christian life.

Understanding what the Bible says about the Holy Spirit will steer believers away from a dead formalism, as well as a mystical or magical view of the work of God. This doctrine of the Holy Spirit is vital to believers who want to know their God better and to serve Him honorably.

13. WE CAN ONLY KNOW GOD THROUGH THE WORK OF THE HOLY SPIRIT

Finally, Scripture says that God wants us to personally know Him. The only One who can correctly explain God is God Himself. God the Son, Jesus Christ, is the One who reveals the Father.

However, Christ is not present with us today. Thus, we need the ministry of God the Holy Spirit to explain who God is, and what He wants from us. This is why the study of the Person of the Holy Spirit is of the utmost importance.

In sum, there are many vital reasons as to why we should study the subject of the Holy Spirit.

SUMMARY TO QUESTION 1
WHY IS IT IMPORTANT TO STUDY THE SUBJECT OF THE HOLY SPIRIT?

The subject of the Holy Spirit is indeed an important one for all believers to study. There are a number of reasons for this.

To begin with, there is a tremendous amount of interest in the subject of the Spirit of God. People are taking the time to examine the doctrine of the Holy Spirit.

Yet there is still an enormous amount of ignorance on the subject. This is an important reason to give this topic serious study.

The doctrine of the Holy Spirit has been a source of division among believers. Understanding what the Scripture has to say on this subject should help end some of that division.

In addition, there is much false doctrine surrounding the Person and work of the Holy Spirit. A systematic study of the Spirit of God should clear up any false teaching.

The subject of the Holy Spirit is dealt with in Scripture, and since all Scripture is profitable, it is profitable to investigate the subject of the Holy Spirit. Add to this, the amount of space the Scripture devotes to the study of the Spirit of God. This makes the subject all the more important to study.

The doctrine of the Holy Spirit is something unique—there is nothing like it in any other religion.

Furthermore, the Holy Spirit is almighty God! Thus, it is imperative that we know more about Him to know more about God.

The Bible says that the Holy Spirit lives inside each believer. Since He is our Teacher, we should learn what we can about Him.

Scripture also says that the Holy Spirit is the One who unifies believers. This makes the study of the Spirit of God essential.

Understanding the Holy Spirit is also imperative for worship. Indeed, He is the God whom we worship.

The study of the Holy Spirit is important for a balanced Christian life. Knowing about Him will keep us from being too legalistic on one hand and too mystical on the other.

Finally, and most important, God wants us to know Him. It was Jesus Christ, God the Son, who revealed God the Father to humanity. Yet the Son is no longer with us. Today, to know who God is, and what He wants from us, we need to understand the ministry of the Holy Spirit in our lives.

It is for these reasons that a study of the Holy Spirit is of vital importance for the Christian.

QUESTION 2

What Is the Proper Way to Approach the Subject of the Spirit of God?

As we begin to study the Person and work of the Holy Spirit there is a proper way for us to approach this all-important subject. Three essential points must be made.

1. THE BIBLE ALONE MUST BE THE GUIDE IN DECIDING THESE ISSUES

First and foremost, although much that is taught with respect to the Holy Spirit is based upon tradition, a particular line of teaching, or a personal experience, the final test must be the Scriptures. We must ask ourselves the question, "What does the Bible have to say about the subject?" Our ultimate goal should be to understand what the Word of God has to say. This takes time and it takes study.

Hence, our view of the Spirit of God should be worked out from studying the entire Scripture. Consequently, we need to be careful about citing one or two texts and then coming to a conclusion. There is the need for finding out what the totality of Scripture says about the Holy Spirit. This is the first important thing we should note.

There Is Room for Legitimate Differences about Some Aspects of the Work of the Holy Spirit

Second, there is also room for believers to have legitimate differences concerning certain aspects of the study of the Spirit of God. Unity among Christians does not mean that we have to agree with one another on every single detail of biblical truth.

Consequently, our view on the subject of God the Holy Spirit should not be used as a test of fellowship, or a way to gauge one's spirituality. There is room for differences.

3. IT IS IMPORTANT TO HAVE A HUMBLE ATTITUDE ABOUT THIS SUBJECT

Finally, it is important that we have an attitude of humility when approaching the subject of the Holy Spirit. We can all learn something new. Unfortunately, there is too much pride that goes along with the subject of the work of the Holy Spirit and spiritual gifts. Such pride is not the work of the Spirit. The Holy Spirit produces the fruit of the Spirit. The Apostle Paul listed the fruit of the Spirit as follows:

> But the fruit of the Spirit is love, joy, peace, patience, kindness, goodness, faithfulness, gentleness, and self-control (Galatians 5:22,23 NET).

These qualities should be the goal of every believer in Jesus Christ. Furthermore, they can only come about through the knowledge of the Person and work of the Holy Spirit.

Consequently, before we study this vital subject we should make certain that we have the proper attitude in our approach.

SUMMARY TO QUESTION 2
WHAT IS THE PROPER WAY TO APPROACH THE SUBJECT OF THE SPIRIT OF GOD?

It is important that we have the right attitude when approaching the subject of the Person and work of the Holy Spirit. Indeed, there are three important things which must be stressed when addressing this matter.

QUESTION 2

Of utmost importance is *where* we derive our information about the Person and work of the Holy Spirit. The Bible, and the Bible alone, should be our only source in coming up with answers to questions about the Spirit of God.

Indeed, tradition and personal experience should not be appealed to in our attempt to answer questions, or solve problems. The final source of authority on all doctrinal matters is the written Word of God. This is particularly true when it comes to the subject of God the Holy Spirit.

There is also room for personal differences among Bible-believers about certain aspects of the ministry of the Holy Spirit. Indeed, there are good Christians who differ on some of the specifics regarding the work of the Spirit. This being the case, we should not assume that we have all the answers with respect to how the Holy Spirit works.

Finally, all of us should exhibit humility when we explore the Person and work of the Spirit of God. There is no place for pride or arrogance when studying about this member of the Godhead.

Each of us has a lot to learn. Consequently, before we look at the subject of God's Spirit we must make certain that we are doing so with the right approach.

QUESTION 3

Why Is the Subject of the Holy Spirit Neglected?

One of the unfortunate things that has happened in the history of the church is the neglect of the study of the Holy Spirit. Unhappily, this is still true today. There are a number of reasons for this. They include the following:

1. THERE ARE OTHER BIBLICAL TEACHINGS THAT ARE SEEMINGLY MORE IMPORTANT

One of the reasons as to why a study of the Holy Spirit has been neglected is because of the perceived importance. While no one doubts the importance of making an in-depth study about the nature of God the Father, or the Person of Jesus Christ, God the Son, the idea of studying about the Holy Spirit has not had the same motivation. His importance is not as obvious as that of God the Father, or the Lord Jesus. Consequently, He is often neglected.

2. THE FATHER AND THE SON ARE OFTEN LINKED WITHOUT THE SPIRIT

We also find that God the Father and God the Son are often linked in Scripture without any mention of the Holy Spirit. Because these two are often associated together, there is the tendency to concentrate on their importance and forget about the importance of the Holy Spirit. This is another cause for His neglect.

3. IT IS OFTEN NEGLECTED FROM THE PULPIT

If teaching concerning the Holy Spirit has not been emphasized from the pulpit, then the great mass of Christians can hardly be blamed for the neglect of the subject. If the leadership puts little or no emphasis on the doctrine of the Holy Spirit, then it is understandable why most Christians would assume the unimportance of the subject.

The experience of many believers would be the same as those disciples that Paul ran into in Ephesus:

> "Did you receive the Holy Spirit when you believed?" he asked them. "No," they replied, "we don't know what you mean. We haven't even heard that there is a Holy Spirit" (Acts 19:2 NLT).

The teaching of the Holy Spirit needs to be proclaimed from the pulpit to remove so much of the ignorance that remains.

4. THERE IS A TENDENCY FOR MAJORING ON THE MINORS

There is also a tendency for believers to "major on the minors." For example, many people are more interested in studying the minute details of Bible prophecy rather than what the Scripture has to say about the Holy Spirit. The desire to know what may, or may not, happen in the future receives more attention than the study of God, Himself.

5. THERE IS A FEAR OF FANATICISM

The subject of the Holy Spirit is often neglected due to a fear of fanaticism. Indeed, since the fanatical behavior of some individuals has been attributed to the Holy Spirit, there is the overreaction of neglecting the Holy Spirit altogether. The fact that the ministry of the Holy Spirit has been the cause for abuse by many well-meaning Christians has caused others to neglect, or ignore, His ministry—lest they be categorized with the "fanatics."

6. THE HOLY SPIRIT IS INVISIBLE

The invisibility of the Holy Spirit is another reason for His neglect. Since the Holy Spirit has no body or shape, He is often thought of in an impersonal or unimportant way. This leads people to ignore or neglect His ministry.

7. HE WORKS INWARDLY NOT OUTWARDLY

The fact that the Holy Spirit works within believers, instead of with some outward display, also causes neglect. There are no great outward signs of His ordinary work. Jesus Christ the Savior did something outward for believers, while the Holy Spirit does things inside believers. This is another cause of neglect.

8. THE HOLY SPIRIT IS HARD FOR US TO CONCEIVE OF

While it is easy to conceive of God the Father and God the Son, it is difficult to conceive of God the Holy Spirit. Jesus was a Person who lived in history. The New Testament gives us many details about His life and ministry. Thus, we can relate to Him.

Likewise, it is easy for us to understand God as an all-wise, all-powerful Father.

However, it is not the same with the Holy Spirit. There is nothing concrete that we can relate to the Spirit, like we can with the Father and God the Son.

9. THE HOLY SPIRIT DOES NOT SPEAK OF HIMSELF

Furthermore, the Holy Spirit does not speak of Himself—He is always representing others. Scripture tells us that He was sent to testify of Jesus. Jesus said:

> I still have many things to say to you, but you cannot bear them now. "However, when He, the Spirit of truth, has

come, He will guide you into all truth; for He will not speak on His own authority, but whatever He hears He will speak; and He will tell you things to come" (John 16:12,13 NKJV).

The fact that He usually works unnoticed contributes to the lack of concern for studying about Him.

10. WE DO NOT HAVE A PERSONAL RELATIONSHIP WITH THE HOLY SPIRIT

While believers have a personal relationship with God the Father through His Son Jesus Christ, there is no such relationship with the Holy Spirit. He is the means through which we know the Father and the Son. We do not have a unique relationship with Him alone.

This is often misunderstood. People will speak of their relationship with the Holy Spirit. Sometimes they pray directly to Him. However, this shows a misunderstanding of the role of the Holy Spirit. He speaks of Jesus Christ—never of Himself. While He may speak to us, we never speak directly to Him.

11. THE RESULT OF NEGLECT IS SPIRITUAL DEADNESS

Unhappily, spiritual deadness has resulted from a neglect of study of the Holy Spirit. This is tragic since the work of Jesus Christ through believers can only come about through the work of the Holy Spirit. Yet there is much opposition to understanding His Person and work from believers for the reasons we just referred to.

Consequently, we should take the time to understand the Person and work of the Holy Spirit. Indeed, this is one subject which should not be ignored!

SUMMARY TO QUESTION 3
WHY IS THE SUBJECT OF THE HOLY SPIRIT NEGLECTED?

Unfortunately, the subject of the Holy Spirit has been neglected by Bible-believing Christians. There are several reasons as to why this is so.

QUESTION 3

For one thing, other teachings have been perceived to be more important than the doctrine of the Holy Spirit. God the Father and Jesus Christ have been assumed to be more crucial for understanding Christian theology. Therefore, we do not study about the Holy Spirit with the same intensity.

Furthermore, God the Father and God the Son are often linked together in Scripture without any mention of the Holy Spirit. This is another reason for the neglect of the study of the Spirit of God.

There has also been a general neglect from the pulpit, which, in turn, has caused neglect by the people.

Unhappily, Christians tend to major on the minors—spending more time on non-essentials than on this important Biblical doctrine.

Add to this, there is also the fear of being classed as a fanatic. Since there are often sensational claims equated with the work of the Holy Spirit from some segments of Christianity, others neglect to study about Him for fear of being linked with these people.

In addition, the Holy Spirit works inwardly and invisibly, which also makes it harder to identify with Him—as opposed to the Father figure of God, or the historical Person of Jesus. Moreover, the mission of the Holy Spirit is to speak of others rather than Himself.

Finally, there is the fact that believers do not have a personal relationship with the Holy Spirit as we do with God the Father and God the Son. His ministry is to testify of Jesus—never Himself.

Each of these factors has led to a general neglect of the subject.

QUESTION 4

Who Is the Holy Spirit? (The Spirit of God)

Before we can answer any specific questions about the Holy Spirit, we must establish a basic understanding of who He is.

The name "Holy Spirit" comes from two Greek words—*hagion*, meaning "holy," and *pneuma*, meaning "spirit." However, the Holy Spirit is known by various names, including the "Spirit of God, the "Spirit of Jesus," the "Spirit of Christ," and the "Spirit of truth." Jesus referred to Him as "another Helper."

There are a couple of basic observations that we need to make about the Spirit of God.

OBSERVATION 1: HE IS A PERSON

The Holy Spirit is not an influence or an impersonal force. He is a person. This can be observed in the following ways in which the Bible speaks of the Holy Spirit.

HE HAS THE CHARACTERISTICS OF A PERSON

The characteristics of the Holy Spirit are those of a person. He thinks, feels, and has a mind. All of the characteristics of personhood are found in the Holy Spirit.

HE ACTS LIKE A PERSON

The Bible describes the Holy Spirit acting as a person. He does the sort of things that only a person can do.

HE IS TREATED AS A PERSON

The Scripture treats the Holy Spirit as a person. Whenever we find the Holy Spirit mentioned in a historical situation He is treated as someone who is personal.

HE HAS A PERSONAL MINISTRY

The office, or ministry, of the Holy Spirit is that of a person. Jesus sent the Holy Spirit to do the same ministry that He was doing while here upon the earth.

HE IS MENTIONED IN CONNECTION WITH OTHER PERSONS

The Holy Spirit is mentioned in connection with other persons. For example, we find Him mentioned with Christians. In addition, we find Him contrasted with personal demonic spirits.

OBSERVATION 2: HE IS A DIVINE PERSON—THE THIRD PERSON OF THE TRINITY

Not only is the Holy Spirit a person, He is a "divine Person." The Bible reveals that God is, by nature, a Trinity. Although only one God exists, there are three distinct "persons" or "centers of consciousness" within the nature of the one God. They are God the Father, God the Son, and God the Holy Spirit.

The Holy Spirit is a distinct Person from God the Father and God the Son, but not a different being. Since the Holy Spirit is the Third Person of the Holy Trinity, He is a divine Person.

THE HOLY SPIRIT IS THE ETERNAL GOD

The Bible makes it clear that the Holy Spirit is not only a Person, He is also God, Himself. We can determine that the Holy Spirit is God in the following ways.

HE IS CALLED GOD

The Holy Spirit is directly called God.

2. HE DOES THINGS ONLY GOD CAN DO

In addition, certain activities that are attributed to God, alone, are attributed to the Holy Spirit. In other words, He does things that only God can do.

3. HE IS TREATED ON AN EQUAL BASIS WITH GOD

The Holy Spirit is treated on an equal basis with God the Father and God the Son. This would be impossible if the Holy Spirit were not God.

HE HAS CHARACTERISTICS THAT BELONG TO GOD ALONE

The Holy Spirit has the characteristics of God. The Bible speaks of the Holy Spirit as all-knowing, everywhere present, all-powerful, and eternal. He is also love, truth and holiness. These characteristics belong only to God.

HE DOES THE WORK OF GOD

The work that the Holy Spirit does belongs to God alone. For example, He is the Creator of the universe, the One who has divinely inspired the Bible, and the One who brought Jesus back from the dead. Only God can do these things.

In sum, as we begin our study of the Holy Spirit we discover two important truths. First, the Holy Spirit is a person, not an impersonal force. Second, the Holy Spirit is God—a member of the Holy Trinity.

We will develop each of these points in the questions that follow.

SUMMARY TO QUESTION 4
WHO IS THE HOLY SPIRIT? (THE SPIRIT OF GOD)

As we begin to study what the Scripture has to say about the Holy Spirit, it is vital to have a general understanding of who He is. The two basics truths about the Holy Spirit, the Spirit of God, are: He is a Person and He is God.

To begin with, the Holy Spirit is not an impersonal force or influence. From a study of Scripture, we will find that He has the characteristics of a person, He acts like a person, He is treated like a person, He has a personal ministry, He is associated with other persons, and He is a divine Person—the Third Person of the Trinity.

Therefore, when we speak of the Holy Spirit we are speaking of one who is a personal being.

Second, the Bible teaches that the Holy Spirit is the eternal God. We discover this in various ways. The Holy Spirit is called God on a number of occasions. Furthermore, the Spirit of God is associated on an equal basis with the God of Scripture.

In addition, He has characteristics that only God has.

Finally, the Spirit of God does things only which God can do.

This is a simple summary of the identity of the Holy Spirit. As we look deeper into the subject of the Spirit of God, we will find that the Scripture, from beginning to end, consistently teaches these truths about Him.

QUESTION 5

Is the Holy Spirit a Person?

To many people, the Holy Spirit is an enigma. Some see Him as an impersonal force or influence, some deny His very existence, and others are not certain who or what the Holy Spirit is. However, the Bible is very clear on this matter; the Holy Spirit is a person, the Third Person of the Holy Trinity.

THE DEFINITION OF PERSON

By "person," we mean one who has their own identity or individuality as a rational being. In other words, they are conscious of their own existence.

When we say that the Holy Spirit is a person, some assume that He has eyes, feet, and hands. But these are not the marks of a person. The marks of a genuine person are knowledge, feelings, and will.

THE HOLY SPIRIT IS A PERSON

The fact that the Holy Spirit is a person can be observed in six ways.

1. He has the characteristics of a person.

2. He acts like a person.

3. He is treated as a person.

4. He has the ministry of a person.

5. He is mentioned in connection with other persons.

6. He is the Third Person of the Trinity, and therefore, is personal.

We will now consider the personhood of the Holy Spirit.

THE HOLY SPIRIT HAS THE CHARACTERISTICS OF A PERSON

The Scriptures attribute to the Holy Spirit characteristics that only a person can truly possess. He is portrayed as a thinking being, a being who has a mind, an emotional being, and a volitional (or choosing) being.

THE HOLY SPIRIT IS A THINKING BEING

The Bible says that the Holy Spirit has the intellectual capacity to think and know. These are the marks of personhood.

The Apostle Paul wrote to the church at Corinth about this aspect of the Spirit of God. He explained it in this manner:

> But we know these things because God has revealed them to us by his Spirit, and his Spirit searches out everything and shows us even God's deep secrets. No one can know what anyone else is really thinking except that person alone, and no one can know God's thoughts except God's own Spirit (1 Corinthians 2:10,11 NLT).

Although no human being can understand the mind of God, the Bible says that Holy Spirit is able to do this. The Holy Spirit thinks, searches, and uses reason. These things imply personality. In fact, the word translated "search" is the same one used by Jesus in John 5:39 where He said the following to the religious leaders:

> You search the Scriptures, for in them you think you have eternal life; and these are they which testify of Me (John 5:39 NKJV).

The word has the idea to "examine or investigate thoroughly." Since the Spirit is said to "search all things" this implies personhood. He searches the deep things of God and reveals them to believers.

THE HOLY SPIRIT HAS A MIND

Scripture also says that the Holy Spirit has a mind. When he wrote his letter to the Romans, the Apostle Paul spoke of the "mind of the spirit:"

> And he who searches our hearts knows the mind of the Spirit, because the Spirit intercedes for God's people in accordance with the will of God (Romans 8:27 NIV).

The word "mind" has the idea of thought and purpose. These are attributes of personhood.

THE HOLY SPIRIT IS AN EMOTIONAL BEING

The Holy Spirit not only thinks like a person, He has feelings like a person. We can give the following examples.

HE CAN GIVE AND RECEIVE LOVE

The Holy Spirit can give and receive love. Paul wrote to the Romans of the love of the Spirit:

> I urge you, brothers and sisters, by our Lord Jesus Christ and by the love of the Spirit, to join me in my struggle by praying to God for me (Romans 15:30 NIV).

The love of Christ can be shown through the love of the Holy Spirit.

THE HOLY SPIRIT CAN BE GRIEVED

He also can be affected by the acts of others—He can be grieved. Isaiah the prophet wrote:

> Then the Lord's people turned against him and made his Holy Spirit sad. So he became their enemy and attacked them (Isaiah 63:10 CEV).

The Holy Spirit is grieved, or made sad, by sin. The fact that He can be grieved demonstrates personhood. Indeed, one cannot grieve, or make sad, an influence or an impersonal force.

THE HOLY SPIRIT CAN BE INSULTED

The Bible says that the Holy Spirit can be insulted. The writer to the Hebrews said:

> How much greater punishment do you think that person deserves who has contempt for the Son of God, and profanes the blood of the covenant that made him holy, and insults the Spirit of grace? (Hebrews 10:29 NET).

The Spirit of God responds emotionally the way that a genuine person responds. Again, this is a sign of personhood.

THE HOLY SPIRIT HAS THE ABILITY TO CHOOSE

After listing the various gifts of the Spirit such as wisdom, knowledge, miracles, and prophecy, Paul links them to the Holy Spirit who gave them.

However, the Holy Spirit not only gives the gifts, He gives them according to His will. The fact that the Holy Spirit has a will to choose shows that He is a person. Paul wrote:

> One and the same Spirit is active in all these, distributing to each person as he wills (1 Corinthians 12:11 CSB).

Notice that the Spirit distributes these gifts according to His will.

The idea that the Holy Spirit has choice is consistent with the character of God. James uses the word "choice" to describe the will of God the Father. He wrote:

By his own choice, he gave us birth by the word of truth so that we would be a kind of firstfruits of his creatures (James 1:18 CSB).

Just as God the Father has a will, so does God the Holy Spirit.

These attributes are consistent with personhood. Therefore, we see that the characteristics ascribed to the Holy Spirit—thought, a mind, feelings, choice—are all attributes of a person.

THE HOLY SPIRIT ACTS LIKE A PERSON

The deeds that the Holy Spirit performs are deeds that only a person can do. His acts and dealings are not those of an impersonal influence or force. There are a number of examples of this.

THE HOLY SPIRIT CAN TEACH OTHERS

The Bible speaks of the Holy Spirit teaching. Paul wrote:

> This is what we speak, not in words taught us by human wisdom but in words taught by the Spirit, explaining spiritual realities with Spirit-taught words (1 Corinthians 2:13 NIV).

It is the Spirit of God who teaches believers about Christ.

Jesus also said that the Holy Spirit would teach believers. Luke records Him saying the following about the teaching ministry of the Spirit:

> For the Holy Spirit will teach you at that time what you should say (Luke 12:12 NIV).

The teaching ministry of the Holy Spirit is an essential part of His ministry.

Jesus said the Holy Spirit would be a teacher of truth. He said:

> But when the Helper comes, whom I shall send to you from the Father, the Spirit of truth who proceeds from the Father,

He will testify of Me. And you also will bear witness, because you have been with Me from the beginning (John 15:26,27 NKJV).

Whatever the Holy Spirit teaches will be truthful. Indeed, as God, He cannot lie.

Jesus also said that the Holy Spirit would teach His disciples "all things:"

> But when the Father sends the Counselor as my representative—and by the Counselor I mean the Holy Spirit—he will teach you everything and will remind you of everything I myself have told you (John 14:26 NLT).

As Jesus taught His disciples, we find that the Holy Spirit would also teach them. He would perform the same type of teaching ministry of Jesus. In fact, He would cause them to remember all things that Christ had earlier taught them. Jesus said:

> But it is actually best for you that I go away, because if I don't, the Counselor won't come. If I do go away, he will come because I will send him to you (John 16:7 NLT).

He personally comes and teaches all believers. This is His responsibility.

THE HOLY SPIRIT GIVES GUIDANCE TO BELIEVERS

The Holy Spirit is a personal guide to Christians. Paul wrote:

> For those who are led by the Spirit of God are the children of God (Romans 8:14 NIV).

God's children are guided by the Holy Spirit.

We find that the Holy Spirit guided Paul into areas of hardship. He gave the following testimony:

> And now, compelled by the Spirit, I am going to Jerusalem, not knowing what will happen to me there. I only know that

in every city the Holy Spirit warns me that prison and hardships are facing me (Acts 20:22,23 NIV).

Thus, the ministry of the Holy Spirit consists of giving guidance to believers.

THE HOLY SPIRIT COMFORTS BELIEVERS

Comforting, or helping, is another ministry of the Holy Spirit. This too is a mark of personhood. On the night of His betrayal, Jesus said the following to His disciples:

> But I tell you that I am going to do what is best for you. That is why I am going away. The Holy Spirit cannot come to help (John 16:7 CEV).

The Holy Spirit comforts, or helps, those who belong to Christ.

THE HOLY SPIRIT GIVES COMMANDS

The Holy Spirit can issue commands that can be obeyed. The Book of Acts records a number of such commands. For example, the Spirit commanded Philip:

> The Spirit told Philip, "Go to that chariot and stay near it" (Acts 8:29 NIV).

The Contemporary English Version translates it this way:

> The Spirit told Philip to catch up with the chariot (Acts 8:29 CEV).

Only a person can issue commands.

Peter was commanded by the Holy Spirit to receive certain men. We read about this incident in the Book of Acts:

> While Peter was still thinking about the vision, the Spirit said to him, "Simon, three men are looking for you. So get

up and go downstairs. Do not hesitate to go with them, for I have sent them" (Acts 10:19,20 NIV).

This is a further indication that the Holy Spirit is a person.

Paul was specifically forbidden by the Holy Spirit to go to Asia. He explained what happened in this manner:

> Paul and his friends went through Phrygia and Galatia, but the Holy Spirit would not let them preach in Asia. After they arrived in Mysia, they tried to go into Bithynia, but the Spirit of Jesus would not let them (Acts 16:6,7 CEV)

In each of these examples, the Holy Spirit commanded them what to do, as well as what not to do.

The Holy Spirit also appoints people to offices in the church. We read the following in the Book of Acts:

> Keep watch over yourselves and all the flock of which the Holy Spirit has made you overseers. Be shepherds of the church of God, which he bought with his own blood (Acts 20:28 NIV).

The Spirit of God appoints people to the ministry of Christ.

THE HOLY SPIRIT GIVES GUIDANCE

Giving guidance is also a work of the Holy Spirit. Jesus said:

> However, when He, the Spirit of truth, has come, He will guide you into all truth; for He will not speak on His own authority, but whatever He hears He will speak; and He will tell you things to come (John 16:13 NKJV).

The Spirit of God was given by the Lord to give guidance to those who believe in Christ.

QUESTION 5

THE HOLY SPIRIT IS ABLE TO SPEAK

The Bible records the Holy Spirit speaking. The Book of Acts records the following:

> While they were worshiping the Lord and going without eating, the Holy Spirit told them, "Appoint Barnabas and Saul to do the work for which I have chosen them" (Acts 13:2 CEV).

The Spirit of God, on occasion, could verbally make Himself known to people.

THE HOLY SPIRIT SPEAKS ON BEHALF OF PEOPLE

The Holy Spirit intercedes, or speaks on behalf of people. Paul wrote:

> Likewise the Spirit also helps in our weaknesses. For we do not know what we should pray for as we ought, but the Spirit Himself makes intercession for us with groanings which cannot be uttered (Romans 8:26 NKJV).

The same Greek word, translated as "intercession," is used later in this chapter of Romans of Christ and His intercessory work. It says:

> Who then is the one who condemns? No one. Christ Jesus who died —more than that, who was raised to life—is at the right hand of God and is also interceding for us (Romans 8:34 NIV).

Hence, both Jesus Christ and the Holy Spirit intercede on behalf of believers.

THE HOLY SPIRIT CAN PERFORM MIRACLES

The Holy Spirit performs miracles. In fact, Jesus Himself said that He cast out demons by the Spirit of God. We read:

> But if it is by the Spirit of God that I drive out demons, then the kingdom of God has come upon you (Matthew 12:28 NIV).

It was through the Spirit of God that Jesus performed miracles.

On the Day of Pentecost, the Holy Spirit miraculously allowed the disciples of Christ to speak in languages previously unlearned. We read about this in the Book of Acts:

> And everyone present was filled with the Holy Spirit and began speaking in other languages, as the Holy Spirit gave them this ability (Acts 2:4 NLT).

Again, we find the Holy Spirit involved in miracles.

The Apostle Paul wrote of the Spirit's miraculous power in his letter to the Romans. He put it this way:

> I have won them over by the miracles done through me as signs from God—all by the power of God's Spirit. In this way, I have fully presented the Good News of Christ all the way from Jerusalem clear over into Illyricum (Romans 15:19 NLT).

Scripture clearly teaches the miraculous working of the Holy Spirit. This too is another sign of the personhood of the Spirit of God.

THE HOLY SPIRIT CONVICTS OF SIN

Conviction of sin is the work of the Holy Spirit. The Lord said the following before the flood in Noah's day:

> Then the LORD said, "My Spirit will not contend with man forever, for he is mortal; his days will be a hundred and twenty years" (Genesis 6:3 NIV).

The Spirit of God will not put up with sin. The fact that this can be said of Him implies personhood.

In fact, Jesus said the Holy Spirit would convict the world of sin. We read His words in the Gospel of John:

> When he [the Holy Spirit] comes, he will prove the world to be in the wrong about sin and righteousness and judgment (John 16:8 NIV).

The Holy Spirit is a Divine Prosecutor convicting the world of its sin.

THE HOLY SPIRIT SETS PEOPLE APART FOR MINISTRY

The Holy Spirit, sanctifies, or sets people apart from ministry. We read the following in the Book of Acts:

> While they were worshiping the Lord and fasting, the Holy Spirit said, "Set apart for me Barnabas and Saul for the work to which I have called them" (Acts 13:2 ESV).

In this instance, it was the Holy Spirit who set these believers apart for God's work.

Peter wrote about the Spirit sanctifying or "setting apart" the believers. He put it this way:

> According to the foreknowledge of God the Father, in the sanctification of the Spirit, for obedience to Jesus Christ and for sprinkling with his blood (1 Peter 1:2 ESV).

People are set apart for God's service by the work of the Spirit of God.

THE HOLY SPIRIT GIVES GIFTS

We are also told that the Holy Spirit gives gifts to believers as He desires. Paul wrote the following to the Corinthians:

> To one is given through the Spirit the utterance of wisdom, and to another the utterance of knowledge according to the same Spirit, to another faith by the same Spirit, to another gifts of healing by the one Spirit, to another the working of miracles, to another prophecy, to another the ability to distinguish between spirits, to another various kinds of tongues, to another the interpretation of tongues. All these are empowered by one and the same Spirit, who apportions to each one individually as he wills (1 Corinthians 12:8-11 ESV).

The Bible makes the distinction between the Holy Spirit and the gifts that He gives to people.

THE HOLY SPIRIT RAISES THE DEAD

The Holy Spirit is also involved in the resurrection of the dead. Paul wrote to the Romans:

> And if the Spirit of him who raised Jesus from the dead is living in you, he who raised Christ from the dead will also give life to your mortal bodies because of his Spirit who lives in you (Romans 8:11 NIV).

The fact that the Spirit of God can raise the dead to life is another indication of His personhood.

THE HOLY SPIRIT CAN CREATE

The Holy Spirit is also the Creator. We read the following in the Book of Genesis:

> Now the earth was formless and empty, darkness was over the surface of the deep, and the Spirit of God was hovering over the waters (Genesis 1:2 NIV).

The Contemporary English Versions says:

The earth was barren, with no form of life; it was under a roaring ocean covered with darkness. But the Spirit of God was moving over the water (Genesis 1:2 CEV).

Hence, we find that the Holy Spirit was intimately involved in the creation process.

THE HOLY SPIRIT IS THE AUTHORITY BEHIND SCRIPTURE

Scripture says that the Holy Spirit is the ultimate authority behind the Bible. Peter wrote:

> For prophecy never had its origin in the will of man, but men spoke from God as they were carried along by the Holy Spirit (2 Peter 1:21 NIV).

These deeds attributed to the Holy Spirit are not the acts of an impersonal force—they are the acts of a person.

THE HOLY SPIRIT IS TREATED AS A PERSON

Whenever the Holy Spirit is encountered in a historical situation we discover that He is always treated as a person.

THE HOLY SPIRIT CAN BE LIED TO

The Bible records that Ananias and Sapphira lied to the Holy Spirit. The Book of Acts says:

> But Peter said, "Ananias, why has Satan filled your heart to lie to the Holy Spirit and keep back part of the price of the land for yourself?" (Acts 5:3 NKJV).

You can lie only to a person.

THE HOLY SPIRIT CAN BE RESISTED

Stephen told the Sanhedrin that they were disobeying the Holy Spirit by resisting Him. We read of him saying:

> You stiff-necked people! Your hearts and ears are still uncircumcised. You are just like your ancestors: You always resist the Holy Spirit! (Acts 7:51 NIV).

You do not disobey an impersonal force—you can only disobey an actual person.

THE HOLY SPIRIT CAN DIRECT PEOPLE

On another occasion Simon Peter went to the house of Cornelius as the Holy Spirit directed. The Book of Acts says:

> And while Peter was pondering the vision, the Spirit said to him, "Behold, three men are looking for you. Rise and go down and accompany them without hesitation, for I have sent them" (Acts 10:19,20 ESV).

Consequently, whenever we find the Holy Spirit in a historical narrative He is consistently treated as though He is a person, never as anything less.

THE HOLY SPIRIT HAS THE MINISTRY OF A PERSON

The Holy Spirit has been given the ministry, or responsibility, that only a person can fulfill. Jesus said that the job of the Holy Spirit was to be another Helper:

> And I will ask the Father, and he will give you another Helper, to be with you forever, even the Spirit of truth, whom the world cannot receive, because it neither sees him nor knows him. You know him, for he dwells with you and will be in you (John 14:16,17 ESV).

The Holy Spirit is "another" Helper. He came to take the place of the absent Savior who is the other Helper. Since Jesus, the first "Helper" is a person, we would also expect the other Helper to also be a person. Indeed, He is.

HE IS ANOTHER HELPER OF THE SAME KIND

We also learn something from the word translated "another." There are two Greek words which can be rendered another—*allos* and *heteros*.

Allos usually means "another of the same kind" while heteros usually means "another of a different kind." The word used here is allos—another of the same kind. The Holy Spirit is another of the same kind of Helper as Jesus—a person.

While the word "another" distinguishes the Holy Spirit from Jesus, it puts the two on the same level. The continuance of the presence of Jesus Christ in the church is because of the Holy Spirit.

THE HOLY SPIRIT IS THE HELPER OR ADVOCATE

The word that is translated "helper" is the Greek word *paraklatos*. The Latin word is *advocatus* in which the English word "advocate" is derived. It has the idea of, "one called to the side of another for the purpose of helping them in any way."

This was particularly true in legal and criminal proceedings. It was the custom in ancient courts for the parties to appear with one or more friends. They were called their *paraklatos*. These people gave their friends their wise counsel as well as speaking and acting on their behalf. All of this was done without charge because the *paraklatos* was concerned for the well-being of the person charged.

THE LORD WAS CONCERNED FOR HIS DISCIPLES

This was the relationship that the Lord Jesus had with His disciples while He was here upon the earth. The disciples were concerned about the idea of Jesus leaving them and going away for good. Christ comforted these men by saying that He was going to send another Helper—the Holy Spirit. The Holy Spirit would defend, help, counsel, and teach them during the time of Jesus' absence from them.

Jesus promised that after He left the world He would not leave His disciples as orphans:

> I will not leave you as orphans; I will come to you (John 14:18 NIV).

The Holy Spirit would take the place of Jesus in His absence.

JESUS MUST GO AWAY FOR THE HELPER TO COME

Jesus said that it was necessary for Him to go away so that the Helper could come. John records the Lord saying the following:

> Nevertheless, I tell you the truth: it is to your advantage that I go away, for if I do not go away, the Helper will not come to you. But if I go, I will send him to you (John 16:7 ESV).

For the Holy Spirit to come, Jesus must go away.

JESUS HIMSELF IS THE HELPER, OR ADVOCATE

Later in Scripture, Jesus Himself is called the Paraklatos, the Advocate (Helper), by John. We read:

> My little children, these things I write to you, so that you may not sin. And if anyone sins, we have an Advocate with the Father, Jesus Christ the righteous (1 John 2:1 NKJV).

The fact that Jesus sent the "Helper" does not mean that He has ceased to be the Helper and Advocate of His people.

Jesus Christ, who is now in heaven, defends the charges made against His people while the Holy Spirit is working the same ministry here on earth. Jesus Christ is the Paraklatos in heaven while the Holy Spirit is the Paraklatos here upon the earth.

THE HOLY SPIRIT WAS SENT IN JESUS' AUTHORITY

There is also the fact that the Holy Spirit is sent in the name, or authority, of Jesus. Christ said:

> But when the Helper comes, whom I will send to you from the Father, the Spirit of truth, who proceeds from the Father, he will bear witness about me. And you also will bear witness, because you have been with me from the beginning (John 15:26-27 ESV).

One does not send some sort of impersonal force or influence in the name of someone to do their work—one sends a person.

We are also told that the Holy Spirit will testify of Jesus Christ and teach the disciples the things they need to know. These are all personal acts.

THE HOLY SPIRIT IS MENTIONED IN CONNECTION WITH OTHER PERSONS

The Holy Spirit is mentioned in connection with other persons. The evidence is as follows.

THE HOLY SPIRIT IS MENTIONED WITH CHRISTIANS

He is mentioned in connection with Christians. The council of Jerusalem wrote the following letter to believers:

> It seemed good to the Holy Spirit and to us not to burden you with anything beyond the following requirements (Acts 15:28 NIV).

Here the Holy Spirit is linked with believers. This of course, implies personhood.

THE HOLY SPIRIT IS MENTIONED WITH JESUS CHRIST

He is also mentioned in connection with Jesus Christ. Jesus said of the Holy Spirit:

> He will bring glory to me by taking from what is mine and making it known to you (John 16:14 NIV).

Jesus mentions the Holy Spirit in connection with Himself. This is further indication of His personal nature.

THE HOLY SPIRIT IS CONNECTED TO GOD THE FATHER AND GOD THE SON

The Holy Spirit is also mentioned in connection with God the Father and God the Son. Paul wrote:

> All the saints greet you. The grace of the Lord Jesus Christ and the love of God and the fellowship of the Holy Spirit be with you all (2 Corinthians 13:13 ESV).

In these contexts, where the Holy Spirit is mentioned, it is alongside genuine persons. There is no hint whatsoever that the Holy Spirit is somehow different in personhood than the other persons mentioned.

THE HOLY SPIRIT IS CONTRASTED TO EVIL SPIRITS

The Bible makes the comparison between the Holy Spirit and evil spirits. Mark wrote:

> But whoever curses the Holy Spirit will never be forgiven. He is guilty of an everlasting sin." Jesus said this because the scribes had said that he had an evil spirit (Mark 3:29-30 God's Word).

The religious leaders claimed that Jesus had an unclean or evil spirit, which allowed Him to cast out demons. In response to the claim that He had an evil spirit, Jesus replied that He had the Holy Spirit. The Lord Jesus said that it the power of the Holy Spirit that allowed Him to cast out the demons.

Furthermore, these evil spirits that Jesus cast out were not impersonal forces—they were personal entities. They have the ability to speak, reason, and show emotion. Contrasting the Holy Spirit to these unclean personal beings is further evidence of the personhood of the Holy Spirit.

THE HOLY SPIRIT IS CONTRASTED WITH DECEIVING SPIRITS

There is also the contrast made between the Holy Spirit and deceitful spirits or demons. We read:

> Now the Spirit expressly says that in later times some will depart from the faith by devoting themselves to deceitful spirits and teachings of demons (1 Timothy 4:1 ESV).

Deceitful spirits, or demons, are treated in the Bible as personal entities. They have the ability to teach things that will cause people to lose faith. In the same manner, the Holy Spirit should be considered a personal being since He is contrasted to them.

In addition, He is said to have "spoken." The ability to speak is a sign of personhood.

HE IS THE SPIRIT THAT GOD GAVE BELIEVERS

There is also the contrast between the Spirit that God gave believers, the Holy Spirit, and false spirits. For example, John wrote:

> Whoever keeps his commandments abides in God, and God in him. And by this we know that he abides in us, by the Spirit whom he has given us (1 John 3:24 ESV).

John then contrasts the Spirit that God gave believers with counterfeit spirits that are claiming to be from God. He said:

> Beloved, do not believe every spirit, but test the spirits to see whether they are from God, for many false prophets have gone out into the world. . . We are from God. Whoever knows God listens to us; whoever is not from God does not listen to us. By this we know the Spirit of truth and the spirit of error (1 John 4:1,6 ESV).

The Spirit of truth, whom God has given to every believer, is personal—just as are these false spirits.

THE HOLY SPIRIT IS PART OF THE GODHEAD

The final reason that we conclude that the Holy Spirit is a person is that He is addressed as God. The evidence is as follows.

THE HOLY SPIRIT IS MENTIONED WITH OTHER MEMBERS OF THE GODHEAD

The Holy Spirit is a member of the Godhead which consists of the Father, the Son, and the Holy Spirit. Jesus said:

> Therefore, go and make disciples of all the nations, baptizing them in the name of the Father and the Son and the Holy Spirit (Matthew 28:19 NLT).

The Father and Son are personal beings. The Holy Spirit is treated in the same manner as they are. In other words, He too is assumed to be a person. Hence, if the Holy Spirit is God, and God is personal, then the Holy Spirit must be personal.

THE HOLY SPIRIT CAN BE BLASPHEMED

Jesus taught that the Holy Spirit could be blasphemed, or dishonored:

> Therefore I tell you, every sin and blasphemy will be forgiven people, but the blasphemy against the Spirit will not be forgiven, And whoever speaks a word against the Son of Man will be forgiven, but whoever speaks against the Holy Spirit will not be forgiven, either in this age or in the age to come (Matthew 12:31,32 ESV).

The unpardonable sin cannot be merely blasphemy against the power of God or some attribute of God. If that were the case, then blasphemy against God Himself would be a lesser offense than blasphemy against His power.

However, the Scripture says that the blasphemy against the Holy Spirit is more serious than the blasphemy against Jesus. This clearly means that the Holy Spirit is personal, and is God.

In sum, the Biblical evidence is beyond dispute—the Holy Spirit is a personal being.

SUMMARY TO QUESTION 5
IS THE HOLY SPIRIT A PERSON?

As we search the Scriptures, we discover that the Holy Spirit is ascribed personhood in the fullest sense. Indeed, through a study of Scripture a number of things become clear. The Holy Spirit has the attributes of a person and He has characteristics that only a genuine person can have.

The Spirit also performs the acts of a person. In other words, He does things that only a person can do.

The Holy Spirit is always treated as a person. In fact, in historical situations the Spirit of God is treated in the same way as other persons are treated.

The Holy Spirit has the ministry of a person. Indeed, He does things in the Christian ministry that only persons can do.

Scripture also mentions the Holy Spirit in connection with other persons. This is further indication that the Spirit of God is indeed a person.

Finally, the Holy Spirit is God, and therefore, by nature, is personal.

To sum up, each of these truths makes it clear that Spirit of God is indeed a person.

QUESTION 6

Does the New Testament Depart from the Normal Rules of Grammar to Indicate the Personhood of the Holy Spirit?

It has been argued that, in a few cases, the New Testament writers depart from the normal rules of grammar to show the personhood of the Holy Spirit. The argument from this can be stated as follows.

THE RULE IN GREEK GRAMMAR

The Greek language has grammatical genders for each noun—they are either masculine, feminine, or neuter. The rule can be simply stated as follows: When a pronoun is used to refer to another noun it must agree with the noun in the same gender.

For example: a neuter noun would have a neuter pronoun referring to it. *Pneuma*, the Greek word translated "Spirit," is a neuter gender word. Therefore, any pronoun that would substitute for *pneuma* would also be in the neuter gender.

It is alleged that what we find in the Gospel of John is a violation of this rule with respect to the Holy Spirit. The writer, the Apostle John, substituted masculine pronouns to show the personhood of the Holy Spirit.

THERE ARE FOUR ALLEGED EXAMPLES IN THE GOSPEL OF JOHN OF THIS VIOLATION

Four passages in the Gospel of John are usually brought up as examples to prove this point. They are as follows:

1. JOHN 14:16,17

In John Chapter 14, we read the following:

> I will ask the Father, and he will give you another helper who will be with you forever. That helper is the Spirit of Truth. The world cannot accept him, because it doesn't see or know him. You know him, because he lives with you and will be in you (John 14:16,17 God's Word).

While the word "Spirit" is in the neuter gender in Greek, the pronouns "Him" and "He" referring to the Holy Spirit are in the masculine gender. Therefore, it is argued that the rules of Greek grammar were violated to emphasize the personhood of the Holy Spirit.

2. JOHN 15:26

It is argued that the same holds true in another passage in John's gospel. Jesus made the following statement:

> "When the Advocate comes, whom I will send to you from the Father —the Spirit of truth who goes out from the Father—he will testify about me (John 15:26 NIV).

Again, we have the words translated "who" and "He" in the masculine, rather than in the neuter gender.

3. JOHN 16:13,14

There is a third example in John 16. It says:

> However, when He, the Spirit of truth, has come, He will guide you into all truth; for He will not speak on His own authority, but whatever He hears He will speak; and He will tell you things to come. "He will glorify Me, for He will take of what is Mine and declare it to you" (John 16:13,14 NKJV).

The word "He" is in the masculine gender.

4. JOHN 16:17

There is a fourth passage where the writer does the same thing. It reads:

> However, I am telling you the truth: It's good for you that I'm going away. If I don't go away, the helper won't come to you. But if I go, I will send him to you (John 16:7 God's Word).

In this fourth instance the word "Him" is masculine in gender, not neuter gender.

The pronoun "He" is in the masculine gender in all these instances. This emphasizes the personhood of the Holy Spirit.

Therefore, it is claimed that these purposeful changes in the Greek grammar emphasize the personhood of the Holy Spirit. There would have been no reason to change from the neuter gender to the masculine gender unless the writer wanted the Holy Spirit to be understood as a person.

RESPONSE TO THIS ARGUMENT

While this argument is often found in books on the Holy Spirit, it is of doubtful merit. It is true that there is a masculine pronoun in these passages that refers to the Holy Spirit.

However, a closer inspection will find that the masculine pronoun does not substitute for the word Spirit "pneuma" but rather to the word for "Helper" (the Greek *paraklatos*). This word is the subject of the sentence and it is masculine in gender.

Therefore, when we find these masculine gender pronouns used in these four passages they are not referring back to the word "Spirit" but rather the word "Helper."

Consequently, no rule of Greek grammar has been violated to emphasize the personhood of the Holy Spirit. The fact that the Holy Spirit is a person is emphasized in other ways.

SUMMARY TO QUESTION 6
DOES THE NEW TESTAMENT DEPART FROM THE NORMAL RULES OF GRAMMAR TO INDICATE THE PERSONHOOD OF THE HOLY SPIRIT?

There is the argument that the Gospel of John breaks the normal rules of Greek grammar by making the pronouns referring to the Holy Spirit in the masculine gender rather than the neuter gender. Four instances are given that supposedly prove this point.

Although this popular argument has made its way into many books on the Holy Spirit, it really does not hold up. The pronouns are not substituting for the Greek word translated as "Spirit" (pneuma) but rather for the Greek word for Helper (paraklatos), which is in the masculine gender. Consequently, no grammatical rule is broken.

This, of course, does not mean that the Holy Spirit is an "it," or is something impersonal. The Bible is clear on this matter. The Holy Spirit is God.

Consequently, He is a personal being. However, we should not use the argument from grammatical gender to prove the point.

QUESTION 7

Could the Holy Spirit Merely be the Personification of God's Power?

There have been those who have argued that the Holy Spirit is not a distinct person from God the Father and God the Son but merely the personification of the power of God. There are a number of reasons as to why this position is put forward.

THE BIBLE OFTEN PERSONIFIES NON-PERSONAL THINGS

The Bible often personifies non-personal things such as wisdom, sin and death, and water and blood. The following are examples of this.

WISDOM IS OFTEN PERSONIFIED IN SCRIPTURE

We find that wisdom is often personified in Scripture. In fact, Jesus illustrated wisdom in this manner. We read the following in Luke:

> But wisdom is proved right by all her children (Luke 7:35 NIV).

In this passage wisdom is said to have children. Of course, wisdom does not have literal children. Consequently, wisdom is personified by Jesus.

SIN AND DEATH ARE OFTEN MADE PERSONAL

Sin and death are said to "have reigned" like a king. Paul used this illustration in his letter to the Romans. He said:

Yet death reigned from Adam to Moses, even over those whose sinning was not like the transgression of Adam, who was a type of the one who was to come (Romans 5:14 ESV).

In this instance, sin and death are treated as something personal.

THE HOLY SPIRIT IS COMPARED TO NON-PERSONAL REALITIES

We also find that the Bible compares the Holy Spirit to realities that are not personal.

1. THE HOLY SPIRIT IS COMPARED TO A DOVE

The fact that the Holy Spirit appeared as a dove is supposedly another indication that He is God's impersonal power:

> As Jesus came out of the water, he saw heaven split open and the Spirit coming down to him as a dove (Mark 1:10 God's Word).

This is used to give evidence of His non-personal nature.

2. THE HOLY SPIRIT IS COMPARED TO FIRE

The Holy Spirit is also compared to fire. John the Baptist is recorded as using this comparison when he said the following about the Holy Spirit:

> I baptize with water those who turn from their sins and turn to God. But someone is coming soon who is far greater than I am—so much greater that I am not even worthy to be his slave. He will baptize you with the Holy Spirit and with fire (Matthew 3:11 NLT).

The Holy Spirit will baptize people with fire.

3. THE FILLING OF THE SPIRIT IS COMPARED TO BEING DRUNK

Scripture compares being filled with the Spirit to getting drunk. Paul wrote the following to the Ephesians:

Don't be drunk with wine, because that will ruin your life. Instead, let the Holy Spirit fill and control you (Ephesians 5:18 NLT).

Since wine is impersonal it is argued that the Spirit is impersonal also.

4. WATER AND BLOOD ARE ALSO PERSONIFIED

Water and blood, along with the Spirit, are called "witnesses." We read the following in the first letter from John:

> For there are three that testify: the Spirit and the water and the blood; and these three agree (1 John 5:7,8 ESV).

Since impersonal realities are often personified in the Bible, it is argued that the Holy Spirit should be seen in the same way. Instead of being a distinct person, the Holy Spirit is seen as the personification of the power or influence of God.

These arguments have convinced some that the Holy Spirit is to be considered God's impersonal power or influence but not a genuine person.

RESPONSE TO THIS ARGUMENT

The idea that the Bible teaches the non-personality of the Holy Spirit does not fit the facts. We can make the following responses to these claims that we have just detailed.

THESE ARE DESCRIPTIONS OF HIS OPERATIONS, NOT HIS CHARACTER

To begin with, the various descriptions of the Holy Spirit, in the passages that we have just considered, are describing the way in which He operates—they are not making a statement about His nature. These are more poetical or descriptive statements of His operations rather than statements of His character. This needs to be understood.

In contrast to this, the passages in which the Holy Spirit is spoken of as a person are not poetical in nature. They are found in sections of Scripture that are either doctrinal or historical narratives. They are not poetry.

THE IMPERSONAL REALITIES ARE WELL-KNOWN

Whenever impersonal realities are personified in Scripture the fact that they are impersonal is well-known to all. Nobody would confuse such things as wisdom, sin, death, or water and blood with something that is personal.

SIN IS IMPERSONAL

In fact, the Bible defines sin in such a way that it is clearly impersonal. Sin is defined as lawlessness, committing acts of unbelief, and failure to do the right thing. John defined it this way in his first letter to the believers:

> Whoever commits sin also commits lawlessness, and sin is lawlessness (1 John 3:4 NKJV).

Sin, therefore, is lawlessness.

The Apostle Paul said whenever we do not act in faith, it is sinful. He wrote the following to the Romans:

> But whoever has doubts is condemned if they eat, because their eating is not from faith; and everything that does not come from faith is sin (Romans 14:23 NIV).

This is another example that sin is impersonal.

James said that if we fail to do something which we know is right we are sinning. He stated it in this manner:

> Whoever knows what is right but doesn't do it is sinning (James 4:17 God's Word).

QUESTION 7

Sin is obviously something impersonal. The Bible makes this clear. Since Scripture nowhere indicates that the Holy Spirit is in the same category as these impersonal realities, then it should be assumed that He indeed is a distinct person.

THESE COMPARISONS SAY NOTHING ABOUT HIS PERSONHOOD

The comparison of the Holy Spirit to non-personal realities such as a dove, fire, and wine says nothing about His Personhood. That line of reasoning would say that the Lord Himself is not a genuine person because He appeared to Moses in a burning bush. However, we read the following account in the Book of Exodus:

> There an angel of the Lord appeared to him from a burning bush. Moses saw that the bush was on fire, but it was not burning up. "This is strange!" he said to himself. "I'll go over and see why the bush isn't burning up." When the Lord saw Moses coming near the bush, he called him by name, and Moses answered, "Here I am" (Exodus 3:2-4 CEV).

The Lord is obviously a personal being!

In addition, fire is also applied figuratively to God Himself. In the Book of Deuteronomy, we read the following:

> The LORD your God is a raging fire, a God who does not tolerate rivals (Deuteronomy 4:24 God's Word).

This does not mean that God is actually made of fire.

In fact, the same letter that tells believers they are to be "filled with the Holy Spirit" also says they are to be, "filled with the fullness of God:"

> And to know the love of Christ that surpasses knowledge, that you may be filled with all the fullness of God (Ephesians 3:19 ESV).

Paul commanded believers to be filled with the Holy Spirit, a personal being, rather than the impersonal substance of wine. He wrote:

> Don't be drunk with wine, because that will ruin your life. Instead, let the Holy Spirit fill and control you (Ephesians 5:18 NLT).

The personal Spirit of God controls believers.

THE HOLY SPIRIT IS DISTINCT FROM THE POWER OF GOD

The Bible makes clear that the Holy Spirit is distinct from God's power. At the announcement of Jesus' conception, the angel Gabriel said to Mary:

> The angel answered, "The Holy Spirit will come down to you, and God's power will come over you. So your child will be called the holy Son of God (Luke 1:35 CEV).

Here the Holy Spirit is spoken of as distinct from God's power.

Jesus ministered in the power of the Spirit:

> Then Jesus returned to Galilee, filled with the Holy Spirit's power. Soon he became well known throughout the surrounding country (Luke 4:14 NLT).

The idea here is that the power came from the Holy Spirit.

6. THE HOLY SPIRIT INTERCEDES FOR BELIEVERS

The Holy Spirit intercedes, or speaks to God, on behalf of believers:

> Likewise the Spirit helps us in our weakness. For we do not know what to pray for as we ought, but the Spirit himself intercedes for us with groanings too deep for words (Romans 8:26 ESV).

If the Holy Spirit were merely God's power, then God would be interceding with Himself.

7. THE HOLY SPIRIT AND THE GIFTS

A distinction is also made between the Holy Spirit and His gifts. Paul wrote the following to the Corinthians:

> There are different kinds of gifts, but the same Spirit distributes them (1 Corinthians 12:4 NIV).

We are one body, with many parts or members.

Paul also wrote to the Corinthians:

> The Spirit gives one person the ability to speak with wisdom. The same Spirit gives another person the ability to speak with knowledge (1 Corinthians 12:8 God's Word).

It is through the Holy Spirit that these gifts are given.

Paul then concluded:

> All these are the work of one and the same Spirit, and he distributes them to each one, just as he determines (1 Corinthians 12:11 NIV).

The Holy Spirit is thus distinguished from His gifts.

MANY PASSAGES WOULD BE NONSENSICAL IF THE HOLY SPIRIT WAS ONLY A POWER

Finally, many passages would be nonsensical if the word "power" or "influence" were substituted for the words "Holy Spirit." For example, we read the following:

> And no doubt you know that God anointed Jesus of Nazareth with the Holy Spirit and with power. Then Jesus

went around doing good and healing all who were oppressed by the Devil, for God was with him (Acts 10:38 NLT).

It would be meaningless to say that God anointed Jesus of Nazareth, "with power and power."

In the letter to the Romans it says:

> Now may the God of hope fill you with all joy and peace as you believe so that you may overflow with hope by the power of the Holy Spirit (Romans 15:13 CSB).

Again, to have the passage read, "by the power of the power" is nonsensical.

In another example, Paul wrote to the Corinthians:

> My speech and my preaching were not with persuasive words of wisdom but with a demonstration of the Spirit's power (1 Corinthians 2:4 CSB).

To make the sentence read, "demonstration of the power and power" would also be meaningless.

From all the evidence, we thus conclude that the Holy Spirit is never described, or equated, with God's power. Indeed, He is a Personal Being, a member of the Godhead—the Holy Trinity.

SUMMARY TO QUESTION 7
COULD THE HOLY SPIRIT MERELY BE THE PERSONIFICATION OF GOD'S POWER?

Some people claim that the Holy Spirit is merely God's power, or the personification of God's power. In other words, He is not a personal being but is actually the power of God.

It is true that the Bible often personifies non-personal things such as wisdom, sin and death, and water and blood.

The Holy Spirit, Himself, is also compared to non-personal realities such as fire. Yet this does not mean that the Holy Spirit is something impersonal.

There is no basis whatsoever for making the Holy Spirit a personification of the power of God. The various comparisons of the Holy Spirit to non-personal realities refer to the way He operates, not His character or nature. Consequently, these comparisons say nothing about the character of the Holy Spirit.

Furthermore, Scripture never describes the Holy Spirit as God's power.

Hence, while such impersonal realities such as wisdom, sin and death, and water and blood are personified in Scripture there is no indication that the Holy Spirit is in the same category.

Finally, attempting to portray the Holy Spirit as merely God's power or influence would make a number of biblical passages nonsensical. This further indicates that Scripture is not attempting to teach us that the Holy Spirit is merely God's power personified.

In fact, He is much so more than that—He is God Himself!

QUESTION 8

Why Is the Holy Spirit Spoken of in the Neuter Gender?

The Greek word translated "spirit" is *pneuma* which means "wind," "breath" or "spirit." Like many languages, Greek attaches gender—masculine, feminine, or neuter—to each noun. The word pneuma is neuter. Does this mean the Holy Spirit is an impersonal force because the word is found in the neuter gender?

1. GRAMMATICAL GENDER IS NOT THE SAME AS PERSONAL GENDER

It must be stressed that grammatical gender is not the same as personal gender. The fact that a word is in the neuter gender has nothing to do with its personal gender. The grammatical gender does not tell us anything about the person nature, or the non-personal nature, of any word. Nothing whatsoever.

2. THE TERM FOR SPIRIT IS FEMININE IN HEBREW AND MASCULINE IN ARAMAIC!

Furthermore, *ruach*, the word for "spirit" in Hebrew, is in the feminine gender! This certainly does not mean the Holy Spirit is a female! The fact that it is in the feminine gender highlights the problem. It is feminine in one language and neuter in another.

But there is more. In Aramaic, the language in which a small portion of Scripture is composed, the word for "spirit" is in the masculine gender!

These three languages are the languages of Holy Scripture. Obviously, they are not trying to teach us something about the personal gender of Holy Spirit.

3. IT DOES NOT SIGNIFY THAT THE HOLY SPIRIT IS AN IMPERSONAL FORCE

Consequently, the neuter gender of the Greek word pneuma does not at all signify that the Holy Spirit is some impersonal neutral force. Based solely upon grammatical gender, one cannot determine, one way or another, whether the Holy Spirit is, or is not, the personal Spirit of God. This has to be decided on other factors.

4. THE HOLY SPIRIT IS NOT MASCULINE

It should also be emphasized that calling the Holy Spirit "He" rather than "it" does not mean He is masculine as opposed to feminine. This is symbolic language. God is neither male nor female in our understanding of the terms. What is emphasized is that He is a Personal Being rather than some impersonal "it" or "thing."

In sum, the fact that the Greek word for spirit, pneuma, is in the neutral gender is not relevant to our discussion on the personhood of the Holy Spirit.

SUMMARY TO QUESTION 8
WHY IS THE HOLY SPIRIT SPOKEN OF IN THE NEUTER GENDER?

The Greek word translated "spirit" in the New Testament is *pneuma*. Interestingly, this noun is in the neuter gender. However, this does not indicate that the Holy Spirit is something impersonal. Indeed, grammatical gender is not the same as personal gender.

In fact, the Hebrew word for spirit, *ruach*, is in the feminine gender. Yet this does not indicate that the Holy Spirit is female. Furthermore, the Aramaic word for spirit is in the masculine gender!

The Holy Spirit is described in Scripture as "He" rather than "it." But this does not indicate that the Holy Spirit is a male as opposed to a female. We use the personal pronoun "He" to describe the Spirit of God because this is how the Bible describes Him—He is a Personal Being.

Thus, the fact that the Greek word for "spirit" is in the neuter gender is a non-issue.

QUESTION 9

Why Do Some Argue That the Holy Spirit Is an Impersonal Force?

There have been those who argue that the Holy Spirit is an impersonal force or influence. They reject the idea that He is a Person.

Sometimes they argue from Scripture while other times they apply so-called logical arguments. However, all of the arguments that are given to prove the non-personhood of the Holy Spirit are all based upon a number of misconceptions. We can make the following observations.

SOME REASONS FOR MISCONCEPTIONS ABOUT THE IDENTITY OF THE HOLY SPIRIT

There are a number of reasons as to why some people have misconceptions concerning the personhood of the Holy Spirit. It is important that we have a correct understanding of the issues involved in order to clear up these misconceptions. This means we need to understand exactly what the Bible does say, or does not say, with respect to the Person of the Holy Spirit.

Some of the most common misconceptions are as follows:

1. THE PERSONHOOD OF THE HOLY SPIRIT IS WRONGLY COMPARED TO HUMAN PERSONALITY

The reason that many people believe that the Holy Spirit is an impersonal force is because they have the wrong starting point. They view the

Holy Spirit from a human perspective to determine whether or not He is personal. The reverse should be true. We should derive our view of personhood from God—not from any view of ourselves.

The argument often goes like this: Since humans are finite, it is assumed that the Holy Spirit must be finite. Since human personality is limited, it is often assumed that for the Holy Spirit to have personality, He, too, must be limited.

However, this does not follow. While perfect personality, or personhood, does not exist in human beings, it does so with God. Humankind was made in the image of God; therefore, any study of personality, or personhood, must begin with God—not with humans.

Our personalities are limited and sinful, while God is infinite and perfect. Therefore, human beings should not be the absolute standard to judge what is and is not true personality. We should look to God for that standard.

2. THE WORD "PERSON" IS AN INADEQUATE TERM TO DESCRIBE GOD'S NATURE

One of the main problems having to do with the study of the Holy Spirit centers around the English word "person." The word does not do justice to all that is involved with God's nature. In fact, everyone admits the word "person" is inadequate to describe what we mean when we speak of God's nature. The problem is there is no better word to describe what we call personality, or personhood. Therefore, the word "person" will have to do.

A simple definition of a person is as follows: A person is one when speaking says, "I," when spoken to is called "you," and when spoken of is called "his" or "her." With this definition in mind, the Holy Spirit clearly qualifies under the definition of a person.

3. THE WORD "SPIRIT" CAN BE TRANSLATED "WIND"

The Holy Spirit is spoken in Scripture as being the "Spirit of God." The word translated "Spirit" can also be translated "breath" or "wind" which implies an unseen impersonal force. This has caused some people to wrongly assume that the Spirit of God is something impersonal.

However, this does not mean that the Holy Spirit is merely "the breath of God." The context must determine whether the writer is speaking poetically of the work of God, or whether he is speaking of the nature or character of the Holy Spirit.

The Scripture uses the symbol of the wind to describe the invisible way that the Holy Spirit works or acts. It does not use it to imply that He is some impersonal influence or force.

4. THE HOLY SPIRIT IS SYMBOLIZED BY IMPERSONAL OBJECTS

Impersonal objects such as wind, water, fire, and oil symbolize the Holy Spirit. Some conclude that this means the Holy Spirit Himself is impersonal. Yet the Scripture also gives many similar symbols for God the Father and God the Son. For example, God is compared to fire:

> For our God is a consuming fire (Hebrews 12:29 KJV).

Though this symbol is used of God, nobody assumes God is to be equated with fire.

Jesus Christ is symbolized as a rock. Paul wrote the following to the Corinthians:

> And all of them drank the same miraculous water. For they all drank from the miraculous rock that traveled with them, and that rock was Christ (1 Corinthians 10:4 NLT).

Again, nobody argues that Jesus is an impersonal being because He is compared to a rock.

In fact, Jesus compared Himself to a gate:

> I am the gate; whoever enters through me will be saved. He will come in and go out, and find pasture (John 10:9 NIV).

Jesus is not claiming to be an actual gate! Consequently, these usages do not mean that God is made of fire, or that Jesus is a rock or a door. These are ways of symbolizing the work of God —they are not descriptions of His basic nature.

Likewise, the similar symbols which are used of the Holy Spirit do not negate His personality. They are describing how He works.

5. THE HOLY SPIRIT HAS NO BODY OR SHAPE

The Holy Spirit has no body or shape. Therefore, He is assumed to be impersonal. Yet personhood is not in any way connected with possessing some physical form. Personhood is based upon intelligence, feeling, and will. It is not based upon whether or not a body is involved.

Neither God, nor angels, nor other supernatural beings that the Lord has created, have any physical form—yet they are personal beings. Therefore, one does not need some type of physical or corporeal form to be considered personal.

6. THE WORK OF THE HOLY SPIRIT IS INVISIBLE

The work of God the Holy Spirit is invisible. This, to some, implies a non-personal entity. The fact, however, that the Holy Spirit is invisible does not mean He is less than a person.

According to Jesus Christ, God the Father is also invisible. He said, "God is Spirit" (John 4:24). Yet God the Father is a personal being. A personal entity does not have to be visible to our eyes.

IT IS HARDER TO RELATE TO THE INVISIBLE SPIRIT OF GOD

It is true that we have a harder time relating to the personhood of the Holy Spirit than to God the Father and God the Son. The titles

"Father" and "Son" generate feelings of personhood to us, while the title "Holy Spirit" is a bit harder to relate. Nevertheless, the Scripture clearly teaches that the Holy Spirit is a Person, despite the fact that He is invisible and has no physical form.

8. THERE IS A FALSE BELIEF THAT THERE IS A DIVINE SPIRIT IN EVERY HUMAN

There is also the popular idea that within each human being, believer and non-believer, there resides some type of "divine spirit." This idea is said to be particularly true of good people.

The impression is then given that the Holy Spirit is merely a name for this higher faculty of human personality. This being the case, the unique personal nature of the Holy Spirit is denied. Yet the Bible does not teach that there is some divine spirit within each and every human being.

9. THOUGH A PERSON, THE HOLY SPIRIT DOES NOT HAVE A PERSONAL RELATIONSHIP WITH HUMANITY

When human beings think of other persons they think of someone who is different from themselves—someone whom we can have a conversation with. However, as far as the Holy Spirit is concerned, He does not act toward us in the same conversational way. He speaks to us, but we never directly speak to Him.

When we relate to the Holy Spirit, it is to relate with God the Father through Jesus Christ. We do not relate with the Spirit of God apart from the Father and the Son. We do not have fellowship, or a relationship, with the Holy Spirit alone. Why? Because His job is to speak about Jesus—it is never to speak about Himself.

While the Holy Spirit is as much of a Person as God the Father and God the Son, as far as relating with humanity is concerned, there is no direct personal relationship. He is the God-appointed means by which we reach the Father and the Son.

SUMMARY TO QUESTION 9
WHY DO SOME ARGUE THAT THE HOLY SPIRIT IS AN IMPERSONAL FORCE?

While the Bible teaches that the Holy Spirit is a personal being, He is considered to be a mere influence or power by some people. There are for a number of reasons as to why this is believed.

For one thing, the limitations of human personality are projected upon the Holy Spirit. Since we are limited, it is wrongfully assumed that the Holy Spirit must also be limited.

The fact that the Holy Spirit is not visible also adds to the idea that He is impersonal. Yet personhood does not have to be linked with visibility. God the Father is invisible, yet He is a personal being.

We also find that the Bible uses impersonal objects to symbolize the Holy Spirit. Yet Scripture also uses such symbols to describe God the Father and God the Son—both of who are personal.

There is also the thought that there is some sort of "divine spirit" that resides inside every human being. Some mistakenly assume this is the Holy Spirit. Scripture teaches no such thing.

Finally, it must be understood that the Holy Spirit does not have a personal relationship with humanity. While there are instances where the Holy Spirit has spoken to humans, there is no record in Scripture of anyone ever directly addressing Him. His ministry is to bring people to Jesus Christ—He does not speak of Himself.

All attempts to make the Holy Spirit an impersonal force or influence do not take into account all the evidence. It is clear from Scripture that the Holy Spirit is a Person—the Third Person of the Holy Trinity.

QUESTION 10

What Do We Learn about the Nature of the Spirit of God from the Old Testament?

The Old Testament records the beginning of God's work with humanity. It also records how the Holy Spirit worked among the people of God as well as in the unbelieving world.

From the Old Testament, there are a number of things that we learn about the Spirit of God. We can make the following observations:

THE SUBJECT OF THE SPIRIT OF GOD IS NOT AS PROMINENT IN THE OLD TESTAMENT

As we examine the pages of the Old Testament, we find that the subject of the Holy Spirit, or the Spirit of God as He is usually called, is not as prominent as in the New Testament. In fact, there are less than one hundred direct references to the Spirit of God in the Old Testament.

THE SPIRIT OF GOD WAS FAMILIAR TO THE PEOPLE

Although the Spirit of God is not mentioned that often in the Old Testament, His existence seems to have been commonly understood and accepted. We find a reference to Him in the second verse of Scripture:

> Now the earth was formless and empty, darkness was over the surface of the deep, and the Spirit of God was hovering over the waters (Genesis 1:2 NIV).

Here we have the Spirit of God mentioned without any explanation. This seems to indicate that the people of the Old Testament era were familiar with the Spirit of God and His works.

3. THE TEACHING ABOUT THE SPIRIT OF GOD IS NOT FULLY DEVELOPED

A fully developed teaching concerning the Spirit of God is not found in the Old Testament. The Old Testament speaks of the Spirit of God as the One who executes God's program. He is the Executor, or the Active Agent of God—the Dynamic Worker of God's will.

As is true in the New Testament, in the Old Testament God is seen to be at work in the world by His Spirit. Whenever we encounter the Spirit of God, something is always happening.

4. THE PERSONHOOD AND DEITY OF THE HOLY SPIRIT ARE NOT DEVELOPED IN THE OLD TESTAMENT

Yet the personhood and the Deity of the Holy Spirit are not developed in the pages of the Old Testament. This is not to say that there are statements in the Old Testament that would deny the personhood and Deity of the Holy Spirit. There are none. It is that the Old Testament does not develop these truths. This is done in the New Testament.

THE NEW TESTAMENT DEVELOPS THE TEACHING ABOUT THE HOLY SPIRIT

The doctrine of the Holy Spirit is more fully developed in the New Testament. However, there is no fundamental difference between the Spirit of God as revealed in the Old Testament, and the Holy Spirit who is active in the New Testament.

The conception of the Holy Spirit in the New Testament is based upon that which is revealed in the Old Testament. In fact, the New Testament doctrine of the Holy Spirit is built upon the teachings of the Old Testament. The martyr Stephen said:

> You stubborn people! You are heathen at heart and deaf to the truth. Must you forever resist the Holy Spirit? But your ancestors did, and so do you! (Acts 7:51 NLT).

The Jewish people understood that it was Holy Spirit whom their ancestors resisted.

Peter wrote about the Old Testament prophets, and precisely what they understood. He put it this way:

> They wondered what the Spirit of Christ within them was talking about when he told them in advance about Christ's suffering and his great glory afterward. They wondered when and to whom all this would happen (1 Peter 1:11 NLT).

The way the Holy Spirit is mentioned in these and other New Testament passages, assumes a direct correlation with the teaching of the Old Testament on the subject.

Therefore, the teaching in Scripture with respect to the Person and work of the Holy Spirit is consistent from beginning to end. Yet the teaching on the subject in the Old Testament is incomplete. It is from the New Testament that this doctrine of the Spirit of God is more fully developed.

SUMMARY TO QUESTION 10
WHAT DO WE LEARN ABOUT THE NATURE OF THE SPIRIT OF GOD FROM THE OLD TESTAMENT?

Though the subject of the Holy Spirit, or the Spirit of God, is not that prominent during the Old Testament period, there are a number of observations which we can make about what was taught.

While not prominent, the Spirit of God was familiar to the people of God. Indeed, He is mentioned on a number of occasions with no explanation about Him whatsoever. This assumes the people who read, or heard the story, had some knowledge of the Spirit of God.

Consequently, as we search the Old Testament we do find that the doctrine of the Holy Spirit is not fully developed. We should not expect it to be. The Bible consists of God progressively revealing Himself to humanity.

Therefore, we find that the doctrines of the personhood and the Deity of the Holy Spirit, while not denied in the Old Testament, are not as developed as they are in the New Testament.

We do, though, find that the New Testament assumes the truth of the Old Testament with respect to the Spirit of God. It develops the doctrine of the Holy Spirit in a thoroughly consistent manner.

In sum, the doctrine of the nature of the Spirit of God, who He truly is, is not fully developed until the New Testament. Yet the Old Testament set the foundation for this all-important doctrine.

QUESTION 11

Is the Holy Spirit Called God?

The Holy Spirit is a Person, but He is also more than that. Indeed, He is Almighty God—the Third Person of the Holy Trinity. The primary reason we believe the Holy Spirit to be God is because the Scripture clearly affirms this. We can make the following observations:

HE IS THE SPIRIT OF GOD AND THE SPIRIT OF THE LORD

In the second verse of the Bible, He is called the Spirit of God. The Book of Genesis puts it in this manner:

> Now the earth was formless and empty, darkness was over the surface of the deep, and the Spirit of God was hovering over the waters (Genesis 1:2 NIV).

It was the Spirit of God, as the Creator, who was hovering over the waters.

The Bible also designates the Holy Spirit as the Spirit of the Lord God, or the Spirit of the Sovereign Lord. Isaiah wrote:

> The Spirit of the Sovereign LORD is on me, because the LORD has anointed me to preach good news to the poor. He has sent me to bind up the brokenhearted, to proclaim freedom for the captives and release from darkness for the prisoners (Isaiah 61:1 NIV).

The Contemporary English Version translates it this way:

> The Spirit of the Lord God has taken control of me! The Lord has chosen and sent me to tell the oppressed the good news, to heal the brokenhearted, and to announce freedom for prisoners and captives (Isaiah 61:1 CEV).

The Holy Spirit is the Spirit of the Lord.

2. HE IS THE GOD OF THE OLD TESTAMENT

A close check of Scripture will show that the Holy Spirit is the God of the Old Testament. There are a number of passages in the Old Testament that says the Lord said or did something. Then, in the New Testament, we discover that it replaces "the Lord" with "the Holy Spirit." We can provide the following illustrations.

ISAIAH HEARD THE VOICE OF THE LORD

For example, we are told that Isaiah the prophet heard the voice of the Lord. We read:

> Then I heard the voice of the Lord saying, "Whom shall I send? And who will go for us?" And I said, "Here am I. Send me!" (Isaiah 6:8 NIV).

It was the actual voice of the Lord that the prophet heard.

THE NEW TESTAMENT SAYS ISAIAH HEARD THE VOICE OF THE HOLY SPIRIT

The New Testament identifies the voice that spoke to Isaiah as the voice of the Holy Spirit. We read the following in the Book of Acts:

> Disagreeing among themselves, they began to leave after Paul made one statement: "The Holy Spirit was right in saying to your ancestors through the prophet Isaiah" (Acts 28:25 CSB).

The Spirit of the Lord is the God of the Old Testament. He is indeed God Himself.

THE PEOPLE GRUMBLED AGAINST THE LORD

The Old Testament says that the people of Israel grumbled against the Lord. Moses wrote about this:

> And in the morning you will see the glory of the LORD, because he has heard your grumbling against him. Who are we, that you should grumble against us? (Exodus 16:7 NIV).

It was the Lord Himself who was the object of this displeasure.

THE PEOPLE GRUMBLED AGAINST THE HOLY SPIRIT

The New Testament, however, says the grumbling of the people was against the Holy Spirit. We read in Hebrews:

> So, as the Holy Spirit says: "Today, if you hear his voice, do not harden your hearts as you did in the rebellion, during the time of testing in the wilderness, where your ancestors tested and tried me, though for forty years they saw what I did" (Hebrews 3:7-9 NIV).

The Holy Spirit is, therefore, the Lord.

ANANIAS AND SAPPHIRA LIED TO GOD, THE HOLY SPIRIT

In the New Testament, we find the following account about Ananias and Sapphira lying to God, the Holy Spirit:

> But a man named Ananias, with his wife Sapphira, sold a piece of property. However, he kept back part of the proceeds with his wife's knowledge, and brought a portion of it and laid it at the apostles' feet.
>
> > "Ananias," Peter asked, "why has Satan filled your heart to lie to the Holy Spirit and keep back part of the proceeds of the

land? Wasn't it yours while you possessed it? And after it was sold, wasn't it at your disposal? Why is it that you planned this thing in your heart? You have not lied to people but to God" (Acts 5:1-4 CSB).

The Apostle Peter made it clear that Ananias did not lie to human beings, but rather to God. However, the Person He lied to was the Holy Spirit. The conclusion is obvious: The Holy Spirit is God.

4. THE LORD IS THE SPIRIT

Paul wrote to the Corinthians and said the Lord is the Spirit. He said:

> Now, the Lord is the Spirit, and wherever the Spirit of the Lord is, he gives freedom (2 Corinthians 3:17 NLT).

It seems that the best way to understand this statement is that the Holy Spirit is the Lord. Consequently, this would be another testimony to the Deity of the Holy Spirit.

THE BODY IS THE TEMPLE OF THE HOLY SPIRIT: IT IS WHERE GOD LIVES

The Apostle Paul says that God's Spirit lives inside the believer. He wrote the following to the Corinthians:

> Don't you realize that all of you together are the temple of God and that the Spirit of God lives in you? (1 Corinthians 3:16 NLT).

God dwells inside of those who have believed in Him.

We are also told that the body of each believer is the temple of the Holy Spirit:

> Or don't you know that your body is the temple of the Holy Spirit, who lives in you and was given to you by God? You do not belong to yourself (1 Corinthians 6:19 NLT).

God dwells within each believer by means of the Holy Spirit—the Third Person of the Holy Trinity.

In sum, as we look at these passages, we find that they clearly teach that the Holy Spirit is indeed the eternal God.

SUMMARY TO QUESTION 11
IS THE HOLY SPIRIT CALLED GOD?

From an investigation of Scripture, we find that the Holy Spirit is the eternal God. There are a number of passages in the Old Testament where certain acts are attributed to the Lord. In the New Testament, these acts are attributed to the Holy Spirit.

For example, we are told that Isaiah heard the voice of the Lord. In the New Testament, when referring to this passage, we are told that Isaiah heard the voice of the Holy Spirit.

The Old Testament tells us that the people of Israel grumbled against the Lord. Again, the New Testament says they grumbled against the Holy Spirit.

Consequently, these examples equate the Holy Spirit with the Lord.

In addition, He is explicitly called God in the New Testament. Ananias and Sapphira were convicted of lying to the Holy Spirit. The Bible specifically says that they lied to God.

We also discover that Paul directly said that the Holy Spirit is the Lord.

Finally, believers are said to be the temple of the Holy Spirit. Elsewhere they are said to be the temple of God. This is another way in which the Holy Spirit is associated with God.

Each of these examples makes it clear that the Holy Spirit is God Himself.

Consequently, He is due the respect and reverence that is directed toward God.

QUESTION 12

Is the Holy Spirit Associated on an Equal Basis with God the Father and God the Son?

As we search the Scripture we find that the Spirit of God, or the Holy Spirit, is called God. Yet there is something else which is important for us to observe. The Holy Spirit is not only called God, He is also associated on an equal basis with the two other members of the Godhead: The Father and the Son. From Scripture, we can make the following observations:

1. THE BAPTISMAL FORMULA THAT JESUS GAVE EQUATES THE THREE

Jesus said that each believer should be baptized in the name of the three members of the Trinity—the Father, the Son, and the Holy Spirit. We read His words in Matthew to His disciples:

> Therefore go and make disciples of all nations, baptizing them in the name of the Father and of the Son and of the Holy Spirit (Matthew 28:19 NIV).

Each believer is to be baptized in the name of the Father, and in the name of the Son, and in the name of the Holy Spirit. The Holy Spirit, therefore, has equal standing to God the Father and God the Son.

Unless the Holy Spirit was equal in nature to the Father and the Son, there is no possibility that He would be equated to them in this manner. This is another indication that the Holy Spirit is God Himself.

THE GREETINGS FROM JOHN MAKES THE THREE PERSONS EQUAL

The Holy Spirit is placed in equal rank with God the Father and God the Son in greetings.

At the beginning of the Book of Revelation we read the following words from John:

> John: To the seven churches in Asia. Grace and peace to you from the one who is, who was, and who is to come, and from the seven spirits before his throne, and from Jesus Christ, the faithful witness, the firstborn from the dead and the ruler of the kings of the earth. To him who loves us and has set us free from our sins by his blood, (Revelation 1:4,5 CSB).

The seven spirits seem to be a reference to the diverse ministry of the Holy Spirit. Again, the Spirit of God is associated with God the Father and God the Son.

3. THE BENEDICTION OF PAUL ASSOCIATES ALL THREE MEMBERS OF THE TRINITY

The Holy Spirit is also linked to God the Father and God the Son in benedictions. The Apostle Paul wrote the following benediction to the Corinthians:

> The grace of the Lord Jesus Christ, and the love of God, and the fellowship of the Holy Spirit be with you all (2 Corinthians 13:13 CSB).

When the Apostle Paul completed his letter to the church of Corinth, he associated the Holy Spirit on an equal basis with God the Father and God the Son. This could only be the case if each of them was equal in character or nature.

Furthermore, the Holy Spirit is listed as a distinct personage from God the Father and God the Son. This is another indication that the Holy Spirit is God Himself, as well as a member of the Holy Trinity.

4. THE WORKINGS OF GOD ASSOCIATE THE HOLY SPIRIT WITH GOD THE FATHER AND GOD THE SON

We also find that the workings of God associate the Holy Spirit equally with God the Father and God the Son. Paul wrote:

> There are diversities of gifts, but the same Spirit. There are differences of ministries, but the same Lord. And there are diversities of activities, but it is the same God who works all in all (1 Corinthians 12:4-6 NKJV).

The Holy Spirit, therefore, is linked, by association, to the other two members of the Godhead. This provides further testimony that they are of the same nature—for neither human beings, nor angels, nor any other supernaturally created beings, are ever associated on the same level with God.

5. THE HOLY SPIRIT APPEARS IN DESCRIPTIONS OF THE TRINITY

The Holy Spirit also appears first in the following description of the members of the Trinity. Paul wrote the following words to the Ephesians:

> There is one body and one Spirit—just as you were called to one hope at your calling—one Lord, one faith, one baptism, one God and Father of all, who is above all and through all and in all (Ephesians 4:4-6 CSB).

This would only happen if the Holy Spirit is equal in character to the two other members of the Godhead.

In another description of the Holy Trinity, the Holy Spirit is mentioned before God the Father. Paul wrote to the Romans:

> I urge you, brothers and sisters, by our Lord Jesus Christ and by the love of the Spirit, to join me in my struggle by praying to God for me (Romans 15:30 NIV).

In sum, the Holy Spirit is the Third Person of the Holy Trinity. He is equal in nature to God the Father and God the Son.

SUMMARY TO QUESTION 12
IS THE HOLY SPIRIT ASSOCIATED ON AN EQUAL BASIS WITH GOD THE FATHER AND GOD THE SON?

The Holy Spirit is not only directly called God, we find that He is also associated on an equal basis with God the Father and God the Son.

We discover this in New Testament baptismal formula. Jesus told His disciples to baptize people in the name of the Father, Son, and Holy Spirit. Each of the three is placed on an equal basis.

The same holds true for greetings. God the Holy Spirit is mentioned together with the Father and the Son.

In his benedictions in certain of his letters, the Apostle Paul linked the Holy Spirit with the Father and the Son. He would not have done this unless they were equal in character.

Furthermore, when God is at work, each of the three members of the Holy Trinity is described as working together. At times, the Holy Spirit is mentioned first—He is listed before God the Father or God the Son. Again, this would be impossible unless they were all equal in nature.

Thus, the Deity of the Holy Spirit is also bound up with the doctrine of the Trinity. If the Deity of the Holy Spirit is rejected, then also the doctrine of the Trinity must be rejected.

On the other hand, if the doctrine of the Trinity is accepted, then one must believe in the Deity of the Holy Spirit.

The Scripture is certainly clear on this matter. Within the nature of the One God there are three distinct Persons: The Father, the Son, and the Holy Spirit.

QUESTION 13

Does the Holy Spirit Have the Attributes of God?

Yes, He does. The attributes of the Holy Spirit are characteristics that God alone has. The following evidence makes this abundantly clear.

1. THE SPIRIT OF GOD IS EVERYWHERE PRESENT (OMNIPRESENT)

The Holy Spirit is said to be "omnipresent" or everywhere present. The psalmist wrote of this important truth. He put it this way:

> Where can I go from your Spirit? Where can I flee from your presence? If I go up to the heavens, you are there; if I make my bed in the depths, you are there. If I rise on the wings of the dawn, if I settle on the far side of the sea, even there your hand will guide me, your right hand will hold me fast (Psalm 139:7-10 NIV).

The Spirit of the Lord is the same as the presence of the Lord. He is everywhere.

Jesus said the Holy Spirit would indwell all believers. We read the following in the gospel of John:

> He is the Holy Spirit, who leads into all truth. The world at large cannot receive him, because it isn't looking for him and doesn't recognize him. But you do, because he lives with you now and later will be in you (John 14:17 NLT).

The fact that He can indwell each of us, at the same time, shows that He is everywhere present.

The Apostle Paul emphasized that all believers were sealed with the Holy Spirit. He stated this in His letter to the Ephesians. He wrote:

> And you also were included in Christ when you heard the word of truth, the gospel of your salvation. When you believed, you were marked in him with a seal, the promised Holy Spirit, who is a deposit guaranteeing our inheritance until the redemption of those who are God's possession—to the praise of his glory (Ephesians 1:13,14 NIV).

This is another testimony that the Spirit of God is everywhere present.

2. HE IS ALL-KNOWING (OMNISCIENT)

The Bible also says the Spirit of God is all knowing, or "omniscient." The Apostle Paul wrote to the Corinthians and made the following statements:

> God's Spirit has shown you everything. His Spirit finds out everything, even what is deep in the mind of God. You are the only one who knows what is in your own mind, and God's Spirit is the only one who knows what is in God's mind (1 Corinthians 2:10,11 CEV).

Someone must be a human being to know things about humans. Likewise, only God can know the intimate things pertaining to God. Since the Holy Spirit knows the things of God, He therefore must be God.

Indeed, the Apostle Paul said that God's ways are unsearchable and unfathomable. He wrote to the Romans:

> God's riches, wisdom, and knowledge are so deep that it is impossible to explain his decisions or to understand his ways (Romans 11:33 God's Word).

Since God's ways are unfathomable to us, but known to the Holy Spirit, this is another indication that the Holy Spirit is God Himself.

The prophet Ezekiel said the following about the Spirit of the Lord:

> Then the Spirit of the LORD came upon me, and he told me to say: "This is what the LORD says: That is what you are saying, O house of Israel, but I know what is going through your mind" (Ezekiel 11:5 NIV).

It is clear the Holy Spirit knows what is in our minds. Only God has this knowledge. Indeed, we are specifically told that God cannot be taught anything new. Isaiah wrote:

> Who has understood the mind of the LORD, or instructed him as his counselor? (Isaiah 40:13 NIV).

Nobody can instruct the Lord because He knows all things.

Jesus said the Holy Spirit is able to teach "all things:"

> But the Helper, the Holy Spirit, whom the Father will send in My name, He will teach you all things, and bring to your remembrance all things that I said to you (John 14:26 NKJV).

Only a being with "all knowledge" could teach "all things."

The Holy Spirit also knows what will happen in the future. Jesus said:

> I have much more to say to you, more than you can now bear. But when he, the Spirit of truth, comes, he will guide you into all the truth. He will not speak on his own; he will speak only what he hears, and he will tell you what is yet to come (John 16:12,13 NIV).

Knowing the future is an attribute that God alone has.

3. HE IS CALLED THE ETERNAL SPIRIT (ETERNALITY)

The eternity of the Holy Spirit is also taught in Scripture. The writer to the Hebrews wrote of the "eternal Spirit:"

> How much more, then, will the blood of Christ, who through the eternal Spirit offered himself unblemished to God, cleanse our consciences from acts that lead to death, so that we may serve the living God! (Hebrews 9:14 NIV).

Eternal existence belongs to God alone. Indeed, every other being has been created at some point in time. The fact that the Holy Spirit is eternal is further evidence of His Deity.

THE HOLY SPIRIT IS ALL-POWERFUL (OMNIPOTENT)

The attribute of being all-powerful, or omnipotent, is also ascribed to the Holy Spirit. In the Book of Job, we read of the Spirit being the Creator:

> The Spirit of God has made me; the breath of the Almighty gives me life (Job 33:4 NIV).

Only God can create life.

In Luke's Gospel, we read again of the Spirit being able to create life. The angel of the Lord said the following to Mary, the mother of Jesus:

> The angel answered, "The Holy Spirit will come on you, and the power of the Most High will overshadow you. So the holy one to be born will be called the Son of God" (Luke 1:35 NIV).

The Holy Spirit has the ability to create life—an attribute of God alone.

5. THE HOLY SPIRIT HAS LIFE IN HIMSELF

Only God has life in Himself. This means that He does not need anything or anyone to exist. We find this attribute in God the Father, God the Son, and God the Holy Spirit.

A. GOD THE FATHER HAS LIFE

The Bible says the Father has life in Himself—He is the living God. As the nation of Israel was about to enter the Promised Land, their leader Joshua emphasized that their God was the "living God." He said:

> Joshua continued, "This is how you will know that the living God is among you and that he will certainly force the Canaanites, Hittites, Hivites, Perizzites, Girgashites, Amorites, and Jebusites out of your way (Joshua 3:10 God's Word).

The God of the Bible is the "living God." Indeed, He is the only God who is alive.

Paul wrote the following to Timothy:

> So that if I can't come for a while, you will know how people must conduct themselves in the household of God. This is the church of the living God, which is the pillar and support of the truth (1 Timothy 3:15 NLT).

He is the living God—the One who has life in Himself.

B. JESUS HAS LIFE

God the Son also has life in Himself. Speaking of Jesus, John wrote the following words:

> In him was life; and the life was the light of men (John 1:4 KJV)

In Jesus, there is life.

Jesus made the following claim about Himself:

> I am the way, the truth, and the life (John 14:6 KJV).

God the Son, Jesus Christ, like God the Father, has life in Himself

C. THE HOLY SPIRIT HAS LIFE IN HIMSELF

The Holy Spirit is called the "Spirit of life," or the "life-giving spirit." Paul wrote:

> For the power of the life-giving Spirit has freed you through Christ Jesus from the power of sin that leads to death (Romans 8:2 NLT).

The Holy Spirit is the life-giver. Therefore, the Holy Spirit, along with the Father and the Son are said to have life in themselves. No other being can claim this.

THE HOLY SPIRIT HAS THE MORAL ATTRIBUTES OF GOD

The Holy Spirit also has moral attributes that belong to God. The Scripture says the following:

A. HE IS THE SPIRIT OF TRUTH

The Holy Spirit is the spirit of truth. Jesus said:

> When the Spirit of truth comes, he will guide you into all truth. He will not be presenting his own ideas; he will be telling you what he has heard. He will tell you about the future (John 16:13 NLT).

Jesus said the Spirit will guide believers into all truth because He is truth. Only God has this particular attribute.

B. THE HOLY SPIRIT HAS THE ATTRIBUTE OF LOVE

The Bible says God is love:

> The one who does not love does not know God, because God is love (1 John 4:8 CSB).

Love is also said to be an attribute of the Spirit of God:

> I urge you, brothers and sisters, by our Lord Jesus Christ and by the love of the Spirit, to join me in my struggle by praying to God for me (Romans 15:30 NIV).

The Holy Spirit can give and receive love.

THE HOLY SPIRIT HAS THE ATTRIBUTE OF HOLINESS

The God of the Bible is holy:

> But as the one who called you is holy, you also are to be holy in all your conduct; for it is written, Be holy, because I am holy (1 Peter 1:15-16 CSB).

The Holy Spirit also has the attribute of holiness:

> Don't give God's Holy Spirit any reason to be upset with you. He has put his seal on you for the day you will be set free {from the world of sin} (Ephesians 4:30 God's Word).

Hence, both the Holy Spirit and God are holy. This is further indication that the Holy Spirit is God.

In sum, these attributes which belong to God alone also belong to the Holy Spirit. Therefore, we can conclude that since the Holy Spirit possesses the attributes or characteristics of God, He is God.

SUMMARY TO QUESTION 13
DOES THE HOLY SPIRIT HAVE THE ATTRIBUTES OF GOD?

The Holy Spirit is directly called God in a number of places in the Bible. However, there is further evidence that He is indeed God. In fact, the same attributes that the Bible ascribes to God are ascribed to the Holy Spirit.

The Bible says that God knows everything. He cannot be taught anything new. Yet the Scripture also says that the Holy Spirit is all-knowing or omniscient. He too knows all things.

The God of Scripture is all-powerful. Nothing is too difficult for Him. Scripture also teaches us that the Holy Spirit is all-powerful. Indeed, nothing is too difficult for Him either.

God is everywhere present in our universe. In other words, one cannot go to some place where God is not there. The Bible says that this is also true of the Holy Spirit. He is everywhere present.

Only the God of the Bible has existed forever. No other being is eternal. The Spirit of God is also said to be eternal.

God alone has life in Himself. The Holy Spirit also has this attribute.

We also find that the moral attributes which belong to God alone are attributes that the Holy Spirit possesses.

For example, the God of Scripture is holy. He is without any sin or imperfection. The Spirit of God, likewise, is holy. There is only righteousness in Him.

God is truth. He does not lie about anything. Indeed, we can be confident that He always speaks the truth. The same can be said for the Holy Spirit. He is called the Spirit of truth.

God is love. We are also told of the love that comes from the Holy Spirit to the believer.

We conclude that the Holy Spirit has attributes that belong to God and to Him alone. Therefore, He is indeed the God of the Bible—the only God who exists.

QUESTION 14

Has the Holy Spirit Performed Divine Works?

The Holy Spirit is a member of the Godhead which consists of God the Father, God the Son, and God the Holy Spirit.

As God, we find that He executes the work of God. Indeed, He performs certain works that only God can perform. We can cite the following evidence:

1. THE HOLY SPIRIT WAS INVOLVED IN THE CREATION OF THE UNIVERSE

The creation of the entire universe was attributed to the Holy Spirit. In the opening chapter of Scripture, we read the following:

> Now the earth was formless and empty, darkness was over the surface of the deep, and the Spirit of God was hovering over the waters (Genesis 1:2 NIV).

Some translations do not see this as a reference to the Holy Spirit but rather of a "wind" sent from God.

The Hebrew word *ruach* can mean "spirit or wind" depending upon the context. Most translations assume that it refers to the Holy Spirit.

In the Book of Job, we are told the beautifying of the heavens was the work of the Spirit of God. We read:

His Spirit made the heavens beautiful, and his power pierced the gliding serpent (Job 26:13 NLT).

It is the Spirit of God who made the heavens beautiful.

The psalmist described the creation in the following manner:

> What a large number of things you have made, O LORD! You made them all by wisdom. The earth is filled with your creatures. The sea is so big and wide with countless creatures, living things both large and small. Ships sail on it, and Leviathan, which you made, plays in it. (Psalm 104:24-26 God's Word).

After describing the creation, which He attributes to the Lord, the psalmist emphasizes that it was the Spirit of God who created everything. He wrote:

> When you send your Spirit, new life is born to replenish all the living of the earth (Psalm 104:30 NLT).

The Holy Spirit is the Creator of all.

2. THE HOLY SPIRIT WAS INVOLVED IN THE CREATION OF LIFE

The Holy Spirit was also involved in the creation of life. Through the Holy Spirit of God, Adam, the first man was created. We read of this in the Book of Genesis:

> Then the Lord God formed a man from the dust of the ground and breathed into his nostrils the breath of life, and the man became a living being (Genesis 2:7 NIV).

The Spirit of God was indeed involved in the creation of life.

The patriarch Job also acknowledged that God's Spirit was involved in the creation of life. He put it this way:

The Spirit of God has made me; the breath of the Almighty gives me life (Job 33:4 NIV).

Again, we have the testimony of this work of the Holy Spirit.

The psalmist also emphasized how the Spirit of God works in creating and renewing "living things." He wrote:

> When you send your Spirit, they are created, and you renew the face of the earth (Psalm 104:30 NIV).

The Holy Spirit creates and renews.

Jesus said the Holy Spirit is the One who gives life:

> It is the Spirit who gives eternal life. Human effort accomplishes nothing. And the very words I have spoken to you are spirit and life (John 6:63 NLT).

Again, creation of life is a work of God alone.

The Apostle Paul wrote about the life-giving Spirit of God:

> And because you belong to him, the power of the life-giving Spirit has freed you from the power of sin that leads to death (Romans 8:2 NLT).

Thus, the Scripture consistently says that Holy Spirit is involved in the creation of life itself.

3. THE HOLY SPIRIT CAN PREDICT THE FUTURE

Only God can accurately predict the future. However, we are told that predictive prophecy is actually done through the Person of the Holy Spirit. Peter wrote:

> Some prophets told how kind God would be to you, and they searched hard to find out more about the way you

would be saved. The Spirit of Christ was in them and was telling them how Christ would suffer and would then be given great honor. So they searched to find out exactly who Christ would be and when this would happen. But they were told that they were serving you and not themselves. They preached to you by the power of the Holy Spirit, who was sent from heaven. And their message was only for you, even though angels would like to know more about it (1 Peter 1:10-12 CEV).

Again, if only God knows the future, and if the Holy Spirit knows the future, then the Holy Spirit must be God.

4. THE HOLY SPIRIT DIVINELY INSPIRED THE BIBLE

The Bible is the written Word of God. We find that God the Holy Spirit is the ultimate source behind the books of the Bible. Peter wrote:

Above all, you must understand that no prophecy of Scripture came about by the prophet's own interpretation of things. For prophecy never had its origin in the human will, but prophets, though human, spoke from God as they were carried along by the Holy Spirit (2 Peter 1:20,21 NIV).

Since God is the ultimate source of Scripture, this is further evidence that the Holy Spirit is indeed God.

In addition, we find that the Apostle Paul tells us that all Scripture is God-breathed. We read:

All Scripture is given by inspiration of God, and is profitable for doctrine, for reproof, for correction, for instruction in righteousness (2 Timothy 3:16 NKJV).

Consequently, the Holy Spirit, the source of biblical truth, must be God.

QUESTION 14

5. THE HOLY SPIRIT TRANSPORTED PEOPLE FROM ONE PLACE TO ANOTHER

We have a number of examples in Scripture where the Holy Spirit supernaturally took believers from one place and brought them to another place.

THE HOLY SPIRIT TRANSPORTED EZEKIEL
This happened three different times to the prophet Ezekiel. We read:

> Then the Spirit lifted me up and brought me to the gate of the house of the LORD that faces east. There at the entrance to the gate were twenty-five men, and I saw among them Jaazaniah son of Azzur and Pelatiah son of Benaiah, leaders of the people (Ezekiel 11:1 NIV).

The Holy Spirit brought the prophet Ezekiel to the temple.

On another occasion, the Lord took Ezekiel to the valley of dry bones. We read:

> The hand of the LORD was upon me, and he brought me out by the Spirit of the LORD and set me in the middle of a valley; it was full of bones (Ezekiel 37:1 NIV)

Again, this is a supernatural work of the Spirit.

On a third occasion, Ezekiel was brought to the inner courtyard of the temple:

> Then the Spirit lifted me up and brought me into the inner court, and the glory of the LORD filled the temple (Ezekiel 43:5 NIV).

Hence, we find the prophet being supernaturally transported on these three occasions. Each time it was by the Spirit of God.

6. ELIJAH SPOKE OF THE ABILITY OF THE SPIRIT TO TRANSPORT SOMEONE

The prophet Elijah thought that the Spirit of the Lord may take the younger prophet Elisha away. He said the following to Elisha:

> But when I leave you, the Spirit of the Lord may carry you off to some place I don't know. Then when I go report to Ahab and he doesn't find you, he will kill me. But I, your servant, have feared the Lord from my youth (1 Kings 18:12 CSB).

Elijah knew that the Spirit of the Lord had this ability.

THE HOLY SPIRIT TOOK ELIJAH AWAY

The Spirit of the Lord then took Elijah away. After this event, some of the people asked the prophet Elisha if they should look for him:

> "There are fifty strong men here with us. Please let them go look for your master. Maybe the Spirit of the Lord carried him off to some mountain or valley." "No," Elisha replied, "they won't find him" (2 Kings 2:16 CEV).

They realized that the Spirit of the Lord had the power to move a person from one place to another. Again, this is a work that only God can do.

PHILIP THE EVANGELIST WAS TRANSPORTED BY THE HOLY SPIRIT

In the New Testament, we find that the Holy Spirit supernaturally brought Philip to another place after speaking to the Ethiopian eunuch. The Bible explains it in this manner:

> When they came up out of the water, the Spirit of the Lord suddenly took Philip away, and the eunuch did not see him again, but went on his way rejoicing. Philip, however, appeared at Azotus and traveled about, preaching the gospel in all the towns until he reached Caesarea (Acts 8:39-40 NIV).

This is another illustration of the Spirit's ability.

This particular capability of the Holy Spirit, to transport people from place to place, is only something that God can do.

7. THE HOLY SPIRIT BROUGHT JESUS CHRIST INTO THE WORLD

The Holy Spirit is the divine agent that brought Jesus, God the Son, into the world. We read of this in the Gospel of Matthew:

> But after he had considered this, an angel of the Lord appeared to him in a dream and said, "Joseph son of David, do not be afraid to take Mary home as your wife, because what is conceived in her is from the Holy Spirit (Matthew 1:20 NIV).

Jesus' birth was a work of the Spirit.

Luke records the same truth. He wrote:

> The angel replied, "The Holy Spirit will come upon you, and the power of the Most High will overshadow you. So the baby born to you will be holy, and he will be called the Son of God" (Luke 1:35 NLT).

The Holy Spirit is the Person who brought about the humanity of Jesus Christ as well as His sinless nature.

Since Jesus Christ has been God from all eternity, He was not brought into being at the time of His human conception. It was only the human form that came into being when He was conceived.

THE HOLY SPIRIT GUIDED JESUS CHRIST THROUGHOUT HIS LIFE

The Bible says that it was the Holy Spirit who guided God the Son, Jesus Christ, during His earthly life. Scripture says:

> Then Jesus returned to Galilee, filled with the Holy Spirit's power. Soon he became well known throughout the surrounding country (Luke 4:14 NLT).

Jesus was guided by the Spirit of God. Only God would have the ability to do this.

THE HOLY SPIRIT BROUGHT JESUS CHRIST BACK FROM THE DEAD

The Bible says that it was the Holy Spirit who brought Jesus Christ back from the dead. The Apostle Paul wrote:

> But if the Spirit of Him who raised Jesus from the dead dwells in you, He who raised Christ from the dead will also give life to your mortal bodies through His Spirit who dwells in you (Romans 8:11 NKJV).

Thus, the resurrection of Christ was a work of the Spirit.

Paul wrote elsewhere that Jesus was raised by the "spirit of holiness." He said:

> And who through the Spirit of holiness was appointed the Son of God in power by his resurrection from the dead: Jesus Christ our Lord. (Romans 1:4 NIV).

Therefore, it was the Spirit of God who brought Jesus back from the dead into His glorified body.

Peter also said that Jesus was made alive by the Spirit:

> For Christ also suffered once for sins, the righteous for the unrighteous, to bring you to God. He was put to death in the body but made alive in the Spirit (1 Peter 3:18 NIV).

Therefore, we have the testimony of Scripture that it is the Spirit of God who brought Jesus back from the dead.

10. THE HOLY SPIRIT REGENERATES THE BELIEVER

The work of regeneration, or giving spiritual life, is attributed to God the Holy Spirit. Paul wrote the following to Titus:

> He saved us, not because of righteous things we had done, but because of his mercy. He saved us through the washing of rebirth and renewal by the Holy Spirit (Titus 3:5 NIV).

It was through the work of the Holy Spirit that we are saved or regenerated.

Jesus Himself taught that the spiritual "new birth" was the work of the Holy Spirit. In a conversation with the religious leader Nicodemus, we read of the Lord saying the following:

> Jesus replied, "The truth is, no one can enter the Kingdom of God without being born of water and the Spirit. Humans can reproduce only human life, but the Holy Spirit gives new life from heaven. So don't be surprised at my statement that you must be born again. Just as you can hear the wind but can't tell where it comes from or where it is going, so you can't explain how people are born of the Spirit" (John 3:5-8 NLT).

It is the Spirit of God who gives life.

11. THE HOLY SPIRIT INTERCEDES FOR BELIEVERS

The Holy Spirit does the divine work of interceding for believers. He speaks to God the Father on our behalf. Paul wrote:

> In the same way, the Spirit helps us in our weakness. We do not know what we ought to pray for, but the Spirit himself intercedes for us through wordless groans (Romans 8:26 NIV).

Thus, one of the works of the Holy Spirit consists of interceding on behalf of the believer. Again, this is a work that only God can do.

12. THE SPIRIT OF GOD SETS BELIEVERS APART FOR GOD'S SERVICE

The Holy Spirit sanctifies, or sets apart, believers for Christian service. Paul wrote the following to the Thessalonians:

> This is why we constantly thank God, because when you received the word of God that you heard from us, you

welcomed it not as a human message, but as it truly is, the word of God, which also works effectively in you who believe (2 Thessalonians 2:13 NKJV).

The setting apart for service is a work of God.

Peter also wrote about the sanctifying, or setting apart, work of the Holy Spirit. He said the following:

> Peter, an apostle of Jesus Christ: To those chosen, living as exiles dispersed abroad in Pontus, Galatia, Cappadocia, Asia, and Bithynia, chosen according to the foreknowledge of God the Father, through the sanctifying work of the Spirit, to be obedient and to be sprinkled with the blood of Jesus Christ. May grace and peace be multiplied to you (1 Peter 1:2 CSB).

The Holy Spirit sets apart the believer for the work of the ministry.

13. THE HOLY SPIRIT HELPS BELIEVERS LIKE JESUS DID

The Holy Spirit presently takes the place of Jesus Christ with earthly believers. Jesus promised this would happen. We read:

> I will ask the Father, and he will give you another helper who will be with you forever. That helper is the Spirit of Truth. The world cannot accept him, because it doesn't see or know him. You know him, because he lives with you and will be in you (John 14:16,17 God's Word).

The Spirit is the Helper. Indeed, He helps us live the way in which we ought to live.

Jesus Christ is pleading the case of believers in heaven while the Holy Spirit is helping the believers upon the earth. John wrote:

> My little children, I am writing you these things so that you may not sin. But if anyone does sin, we have an advocate

with the Father— Jesus Christ the righteous one (1 John 2:1 CSB).

The Holy Spirit helps believers in the same way as Jesus did.

CONCLUSION: THE HOLY SPIRIT DOES THINGS ONLY GOD CAN DO

Each of these many works are works of God; for there is no being less than God that can perform them. Since the Holy Spirit does things only God can do—He too must be God.

SUMMARY TO QUESTION 14
HAS THE HOLY SPIRIT PERFORMED DIVINE WORKS?

The Holy Spirit is God. There are a number of different ways in which we know this. For one thing, the Bible attributes various works to the Holy Spirit that belong to God and Him alone. They include the following.

The creation of the heaven and the earth is a work of God. According to Scripture, it is also a work of the Holy Spirit.

The creation of life is something which God alone has the power of doing. Yet we are told that the Spirit of God creates life. Indeed, He was involved in the creation of the first man, Adam.

The Bible says that God alone predicts the future accurately. Indeed, no other being in the universe can know what will happen in the future. The Scripture also tells us that it is the Holy Spirit who predicts the future. Thus, He must be God.

The Holy Spirit is the One who divinely inspired the Bible. The Bible also makes it clear that God is the source of Scripture. Again, we conclude, the Holy Spirit must be God.

The New Testament says that Jesus Christ was brought into our world by the Holy Spirit. This too is a work of God.

It was the Spirit of the Lord who guided Jesus Christ throughout His earthly life and ministry. Only God could do something like this.

Scripture says that the Holy Spirit brought Jesus back from the dead. In another place, it tells us that God brought Jesus back from the dead. Therefore, the Holy Spirit must indeed be God.

The Bible also says that regenerating, or giving spiritual life to every believer, is a work of the Spirit of God. It is a work that only God can do.

The Holy Spirit is the One who intercedes to God on behalf of each believer. No human is able to do this.

The Spirit of God also sets apart believers for God's service. This too is a work of God alone.

The Spirit of the Lord helps believers become like Jesus Christ. This is a supernatural work of the Lord—something only God can do

Consequently, the evidence clearly demonstrates that the Holy Spirit is God Himself.

QUESTION 15

What Different Titles Are Ascribed To the Spirit of God?

As we study the Scripture, we find that the Spirit of God is never given a formal name, such as we have with God the Son—who was given the name Jesus.

However, no such name is ever given to the Holy Spirit. Instead, we find that the Third Person of the Trinity is designated by a number of titles.

THE SPIRIT OF GOD

The most common title in the Old Testament is the Spirit of God, or the Spirit of the Lord. In the second verse of the Bible we find Him called the "Spirit of God:"

> Now the earth was formless and empty, darkness covered the surface of the watery depths, and the Spirit of God was hovering over the surface of the waters (Genesis 1:2 CSB).

When He is first introduced to us in the Bible, He is referred to as the "Spirit of God."

THE SPIRIT OF THE LORD

Isaiah the prophet uses the title "Spirit of the Lord" when describing Him. We read:

Like cattle that go down to the plain, they were given rest by the Spirit of the LORD. This is how you guided your people to make for yourself a glorious name (Isaiah 63:14 NIV).

Therefore, He is called both the "Spirit of God," as well as the "Spirit of the Lord."

THE HOLY SPIRIT

The most common title found in the New Testament is the Holy Spirit. Jesus said the following about Him.

> If you then, being evil, know how to give good gifts to your children, how much more will your heavenly Father give the Holy Spirit to those who ask Him! (Luke 11:13 NKJV).

He is called "Holy" because He is the Spirit of the Holy One.

THE SPIRIT

The "Spirit" is another common designation for the Third Person of the Trinity in the New Testament. Jesus said:

> Flesh gives birth to flesh, but the Spirit gives birth to spirit. You should not be surprised at my saying, 'You must be born again.' The wind blows wherever it pleases. You hear its sound, but you cannot tell where it comes from or where it is going. So it is with everyone born of the Spirit" (John 3:6-8 NIV).

The New Living Translation says:

> Humans can reproduce only human life, but the Holy Spirit gives new life from heaven. So don't be surprised at my statement that you must be born again. Just as you can hear the wind but can't tell where it comes from or where it is going, so you can't explain how people are born of the Spirit (John 3:6-8 NLT).

QUESTION 15

Thus, sometimes He is referred to as the "Spirit."

THE TITLES CAN BE PLACED INTO THREE BASIC CATEGORIES

The titles of the Spirit of God, or the Holy Spirit, can be simply placed into three basic categories. They include the following:

1. There are titles that show how He relates to God the Father.

2. Other titles relate Him to God the Son.

3. There are other titles that reflect His divine attributes and divine works.

TITLES THAT RELATE THE SPIRIT OF GOD TO THE FATHER

Some of the titles of the Holy Spirit reveal His relationship to God the Father. They include the following:

1. THE SPIRIT OF GOD

Paul uses the term the "Spirit of God" when referring to the Third Person of the Trinity:

> Do you not know that you are the temple of God and that the Spirit of God dwells in you? (1 Corinthians 3:16 NKJV)

He is the Spirit of God, or the Spirit who comes from God the Father.

2. THE HOLY SPIRIT OF GOD

The "Holy Spirit of God" is another designation. This emphasizes that He is somehow related to God the Father. Paul wrote:

> And do not grieve the Holy Spirit of God, with whom you were sealed for the day of redemption (Ephesians 4:30 NIV).

He is the Holy Spirit of God.

3. SPIRIT OF OUR GOD

Paul calls Him the "Spirit of our God" when he wrote to the Corinthians. "Our God" would refer to God the Father:

> And that is what some of you were. But you were washed, you were sanctified, you were justified in the name of the Lord Jesus Christ and by the Spirit of our God (1 Corinthians 6:11 NIV).

The Spirit is the Spirit of our God.

4. HIS SPIRIT

He is called "His Spirit:"

> But Moses asked him, "Do you think you need to stand up for me? I wish all the Lord's people were prophets and that the Lord would put his Spirit on them" (Numbers 11:29 God's Word).

Again, this is likely a reference to God the Father.

5. THE SPIRIT OF THE LORD GOD

Isaiah uses the term "Spirit of the Lord God:"

> The Spirit of the Lord God is on me, because the Lord has anointed me to bring good news to the poor. He has sent me to heal the brokenhearted, to proclaim liberty to the captives and freedom to the prisoners (Isaiah 61:1 CSB).

This is also translated as the "Spirit of the Sovereign Lord." The New International Version puts it this way:

> The Spirit of the Sovereign LORD is on me, because the LORD has anointed me to preach good news to the poor. He has sent me to bind up the brokenhearted, to proclaim

freedom for the captives and release from darkness for the prisoners (Isaiah 61:1 NIV).

This verse was quoted by Jesus in the New Testament when He said that the Spirit of the Lord was upon Him:

> The Spirit of the Lord is on me, because he has anointed me to proclaim good news to the poor (Luke 4:18 NIV).

This reference also links the Holy Spirit with God the Father.

6. THE SPIRIT OF THE LIVING GOD

The "Spirit of the Living God" is a term used by Paul:

> You are like a letter written by Christ and delivered by us. But you are not written with pen and ink or on tablets made of stone. You are written in our hearts by the Spirit of the living God (2 Corinthians 3:3 CEV).

This again emphasizes that the God of Scripture is the Living God.

7. THE SPIRIT OF YOUR FATHER

Jesus specifically called the Holy Spirit "the Spirit of your Father." Christ did this when He was instructing His disciples about what to say when confronted by opposition. We read His words to them:

> For it won't be you doing the talking—it will be the Spirit of your Father speaking through you (Matthew 10:20 NLT).

Each of these titles shows that there is a personal relationship between God the Father and the Holy Spirit.

THERE ARE TITLES THAT RELATE HIM TO JESUS, GOD THE SON

Some of the titles of the Holy Spirit relate Him to God the Son, Jesus Christ. They are as follows:

1. THE SPIRIT OF JESUS

Paul used the term "the Spirit of Jesus" when referring to God's Spirit:

> Paul and his friends went through Phrygia and Galatia, but the Holy Spirit would not let them preach in Asia. After they arrived in Mysia, they tried to go into Bithynia, but the Spirit of Jesus would not let them (Acts 16:6,7 CEV).

The Holy Spirit is the Spirit of Jesus. This means that He is the Spirit whom Jesus sends to the world to represent Him while He is in heaven.

2. THE SPIRIT OF CHRIST

Paul also uses the term the "Spirit of Christ" when he referred to the Holy Spirit. He wrote the following to the Romans:

> You, however, are not controlled by the sinful nature but are in the Spirit, if indeed the Spirit of God lives in you. And if anyone does not have the Spirit of Christ, they do not belong to Christ (Romans 8:9 NIV).

The Holy Spirit is the "Spirit of Christ."

3. THE SPIRIT OF JESUS CHRIST

Paul also speaks of the "Spirit of Jesus Christ." He wrote the following in the first chapter of his letter to the church of Philippi:

> For I know that through your prayers and God's provision of the Spirit of Jesus Christ what has happened to me will turn out for my deliverance (Philippians 1:19 NIV).

The Spirit of God is the Spirit of Jesus Christ. Again, He is the Spirit which represents Christ while Jesus is no longer upon the earth.

4. THE SPIRIT OF HIS SON

The Holy Spirit is also called the "Spirit of His Son:"

And because you are sons, God has sent forth the Spirit of His Son into your hearts, crying out, "Abba, Father!" (Galatians 4:6 NKJV).

The Holy Spirit is the Spirit of His son. This further links the Holy Spirit with Jesus.

5. THE SPIRIT OF THE LORD

The Spirit of God is called the "Spirit of the Lord:"

Then Peter said to her, "How could you and your husband agree to test the Lord's Spirit? Those who buried your husband are standing at the door, and they will carry you outside for burial" (Acts 5:9 God's Word).

In this context, the Lord seems to refer to Jesus.

THERE ARE TITLES THAT RELATE TO HIS DIVINE ATTRIBUTES AND DIVINE WORKS

There are a number of titles of the Holy Spirit that reveal His divine attributes, as well as His divine works, further confirming He is God—the Third Person of the Holy Trinity.

1. THE SPIRIT WHO IS FROM GOD

He is also designated "the Spirit who is from God." The Apostle Paul stated the following in his letter to the Corinthians:

And God has actually given us his Spirit (not the world's spirit) so we can know the wonderful things God has freely given us (1 Corinthians 2:12 NLT).

He is the Spirit who is from God.

2. THE SPIRIT OF LIFE

Paul called Him the "Spirit of life." Paul wrote to the Romans:

> For the power of the life-giving Spirit has freed you through Christ Jesus from the power of sin that leads to death (Romans 8:2 NLT).

The Spirit of God is the Spirit of life. Only God can give life.

3. THE SPIRIT OF TRUTH

Jesus called the Holy Spirit the "Spirit of truth."

> The Spirit of truth, whom the world cannot receive, because it neither sees Him nor knows Him; but you know Him, for He dwells with you and will be in you (John 14:17 NKJV).

The Holy Spirit is the Spirit of truth.

4. THE SPIRIT OF GLORY

Peter refers to the Spirit of God as the "Spirit of glory." He wrote:

> If you are insulted because of the name of Christ, you are blessed, for the Spirit of glory and of God rests on you (1 Peter 4:14 NIV).

Glory belongs to God alone.

5. THE LORD, THE SPIRIT

Paul called the Holy Spirit, "the Lord, the Spirit." He wrote:

> We all, with unveiled faces, are looking as in a mirror at the glory of the Lord and are being transformed into the same image from glory to glory; this is from the Lord who is the Spirit (2 Corinthians 3:18 CSB).

He is the Lord, the Spirit.

6. THE SPIRIT OF HOLINESS

The title "the Spirit of Holiness" is used to describe the Holy Spirit. Speaking of Jesus, Paul wrote the following to the Romans:

And was appointed to be the powerful Son of God according to the Spirit of holiness by the resurrection of the dead (Romans 1:4 CSB).

The Holy Spirit is indeed the Spirit of holiness.

7. THE HOLY ONE

John, in his first letter to the believers, calls the Holy Spirit the "Holy One." He wrote:

> But you have an anointing from the Holy One, and all of you know the truth (1 John 2:20 NIV).

Only God is holy.

8. THE SPIRIT OF GRACE

The writer to the Hebrews calls Him "the Spirit of grace." The writer to the Hebrews puts it in this manner:

> How much more severely do you think someone deserves to be punished who has trampled the Son of God underfoot, who has treated as an unholy thing the blood of the covenant that sanctified them, and who has insulted the Spirit of grace? (Hebrews 10:29 NIV).

The Lord is the only One who can be gracious to sinners.

9. THE SEVEN SPIRITS

The Holy Spirit is called the "seven Spirits." We read of this in the Book of Revelation:

> John to the seven churches that are in Asia: Grace to you and peace from him who is and who was and who is to come, and from the seven spirits who are before his throne (Revelation 1:4 ESV).

The number seven speaks of completion or fullness.

10. THE GOOD SPIRIT

In the Book of Nehemiah, we find the Holy Spirit referred to as "the good Spirit." Scripture says the following:

> You sent your good Spirit to instruct them, and you did not stop giving them bread from heaven or water for their thirst (Nehemiah 9:20 NLT).

He is indeed the "good Spirit."

Jesus made it clear that no one is good but God:

> Once a religious leader asked Jesus this question: "Good teacher, what should I do to get eternal life?" "Why do you call me good?" Jesus asked him. "Only God is truly good" (Luke 18:18,19 NLT).

The Holy Spirit is God.

11. THE SPIRIT OF GRACE AND SUPPLICATION

He is also known as the "Spirit of grace and supplication." The prophet Zechariah recorded the Lord saying the following:

> And I will pour out on the house of David and the inhabitants of Jerusalem a spirit of grace and supplication. They will look on me, the one they have pierced, and they will mourn for him as one mourns for an only child, and grieve bitterly for him as one grieves for a firstborn son (Zechariah 12:10 NIV).

The Holy Spirit is the Spirit of grace.

12. THE SPIRIT OF ADOPTION (SONSHIP)

The Holy Spirit is called the "Spirit of adoption" or "Sonship:"

> For you did not receive the spirit of slavery to fall back into fear, but you have received the Spirit of adoption as sons, by whom we cry, "Abba! Father!" (Romans 8:15 ESV).

It is the Spirit of God who adopts us into the family of God.

Consequently, these titles used of the Holy Spirit are another indication that He is in fact the Third Person of the Trinity. Indeed, only God could be given titles such as He, the Holy Spirit, has been given.

SUMMARY TO QUESTION 15
WHAT DIFFERENT TITLES ARE ASCRIBED TO THE SPIRIT OF GOD?

While God the Son has the formal name of Jesus Christ, there is no formal name for the Third Person of the Trinity. Instead, He is known by a number of titles.

The most common title in the Old Testament is the "Spirit of God," or the "Spirit of the Lord." The most common title in the New Testament is the "Holy Spirit." The various titles given to the Holy Spirit can be placed into three simple categories.

First, there are titles that show His relationship with God the Father. When we examine them, we find that there is an intimate relationship between the Father and the Spirit.

Next, there are titles that reflect His relationship to God the Son. Again, we find that an intimate relationship exists between the Son and the Spirit. This is further evidence that they are of the same essence.

Finally, there are titles of the Spirit of God that show His divine attributes, as well as His divine works. Indeed, these titles could never be used of any being less than God.

In sum, these titles make it clear that the Spirit of God is God Himself—the Third Person of the Holy Trinity. Consequently, they provide further evidence of the Deity of God the Holy Spirit.

QUESTION 16

Should the Holy Spirit Be Singled out for Worship?

Since the Holy Spirit is God, should He be singled out for worship? What does the Bible have to say about this issue?

OPTION 1: SOME BELIEVE THE HOLY SPIRIT SHOULD BE SINGLED OUT FOR WORSHIP

There are some believers who think that the Holy Spirit should indeed be singled out for worship. They argue that the historic church has practiced worship of the Holy Spirit.

In fact, there are preserved prayers to the Holy Spirit from the fourth century until today. The Orthodox Church, the Roman Catholic Church, and most mainline Protestant denominations, still use hymns and prayers to the Holy Spirit. Therefore, it is argued, that we should single out the Holy Spirit for worship.

DOES THE BIBLE COMMAND BELIEVERS TO WORSHIP THE SPIRIT?

Some have argued that the New Testament may command the worship of the Holy Spirit. They cite one possible translation of Philippians 3:3 which says that we do worship the Holy Spirit. It reads as follows:

> For we are the circumcision, who worship the Spirit of God (Philippians 3:3).

If this is the correct understanding of this verse, then it would be a direct statement that believers do worship of the Holy Spirit.

Consequently, worship of the Holy Spirit is something that believers think they should practice because the Bible allows for it.

Option 2: Believers Do Not Single out the Holy Spirit for Worship

While some think the Holy Spirit should be singled out for worship, the Bible says that the Holy Spirit's job is not glorifying Himself. Indeed, it is the mission of the Holy Spirit to glorify Jesus Christ. Jesus made this clear when He said the following:

> But when the Helper comes, whom I shall send to you from the Father, the Spirit of truth who proceeds from the Father, He will testify of Me (John 15:26 NKJV).

Jesus said that the Holy Spirit is to testify of Him.

Jesus repeated this same truth later. Again, He said:

> When the Spirit of truth comes, he will guide you into all truth. He will not be presenting his own ideas; he will be telling you what he has heard. He will tell you about the future. He will bring me glory by revealing to you whatever he receives from me (John 16:13,14 NLT).

The Bible is clear. Jesus sent the Holy Spirit Jesus to speak of Himself. We do not have a personal relationship with the Spirit of God as we do with Jesus Christ. Therefore, worship of the Holy Spirit is not something that believers should practice.

In addition, the possible translation of Philippians 3:3, where the command is to worship the Spirit, is not found in any major translation of Scripture. Most translations render this verse as follows.

> For we who worship God in the Spirit are the only ones who are truly circumcised. We put no confidence in human effort. Instead, we boast about what Christ Jesus has done for us (Philippians 3:3 NLT)

The usual translation does not teach that we single out the Holy Spirit for worship. Instead, it says that we worship God "in the Spirit" or "by the Spirit." However, we do not single out the Holy Spirit for worship.

DOES THIS MEAN THAT WE DO NOT WORSHIP THE HOLY SPIRIT?

Does this mean we should not worship the Holy Spirit at all? Though some would say we should not, the fact is that we do worship the Holy Spirit.

While there may be no direct commandments to single out the Holy Spirit for worship, we do worship Him when we worship God because the Holy Spirit is God. To deny worship to the Holy Spirit is to deny His Deity.

Therefore, it is proper to say that we do worship the Holy Spirit when we worship God in Trinity. Yet it is also true that we should not single out the Holy Spirit for worship.

SUMMARY TO QUESTION 16
SHOULD THE HOLY SPIRIT BE SINGLED OUT FOR WORSHIP?

There is a question as to whether or not we should single out the Holy Spirit, the Third Person of the Trinity, for worship. Christians differ on this.

Some believe that the Holy Spirit, since He is God, should be singled out for worship. They believe there is nothing wrong with worshipping the Holy Spirit without mentioning God the Father or God the Son.

In fact, one possible translation of Philippians 3:3 says that we do worship the Holy Spirit. Consequently, there is nothing improper about singling out the Holy Spirit for worship.

However, the Holy Spirit is not singled out for worship in the New Testament. His ministry is not to speak of Himself—His mission is to speak about Jesus Christ. Jesus made this clear. He said the responsibility of the Holy Spirit was to draw attention to Jesus, not to Himself.

Indeed, Jesus specifically said that the Holy Spirit would not speak of Himself. Thus, it is wrong to single Him out for worship.

In addition, there is no specific command to worship Him alone. The translation that some offer of Philippians 3:3, which they say acknowledged the Holy Spirit is singled out for worship, is not a legitimate alternative to the traditional understanding of the verse. Rather it says that we worship God "by means of the Holy Spirit."

Therefore, the Spirit of God should not be the sole object of our worship.

However, we do worship the Holy Spirit when we worship God since He is the Third Person of the Trinity. He is indeed worthy of our worship as part of the Godhead. Yet we should not single Him out for worship. Scripture is clear on this issue.

QUESTION 17

Whom Does the Holy Spirit Proceed From? (Procession, Filioque Controversy)

An issue that has troubled the church is in regard to the procession of the Holy Spirit. The word "procession" concerns the relationship of the Holy Spirit with respect to God the Father and God the Son.

DOES THE HOLY SPIRIT PROCEED FROM GOD THE FATHER, OR FROM GOD THE FATHER AND GOD THE SON?

As we shall see, while this may not seem like a very important matter, it has had enormous consequences in the history of the church. A number of observations need to be made:

THE FATHER SENDS THE HOLY SPIRIT

There is a passage that says God the Father is the One who sends the Holy Spirit. Jesus Himself said this. We read His statement in John's gospel:

All this I have spoken while still with you. But the Advocate, the Holy Spirit, whom the Father will send in my name, will teach you all things and will remind you of everything I have said to you (John 14:26 NIV).

According to Jesus, the Holy Spirit will be sent by the Father.

THE HOLY SPIRIT IS SENT FROM JESUS

Yet there is another passage that affirms that the Holy Spirit will be sent from Jesus. Christ made the following statement after He had risen from the dead:

> I am going to send you what my Father has promised; but stay in the city until you have been clothed with power from on high (Luke 24:49 NIV).

Here it is Jesus who is sending the Holy Spirit.

THE HOLY SPIRIT PROCEEDS FROM BOTH THE FATHER AND THE SON

This problem is seemingly solved when we look at another statement of Jesus. In John's gospel, Jesus indicates the Holy Spirit proceeds from both God the Father and God the Son. Jesus again said:

> When the Counselor comes, the one I will send to you from the Father—the Spirit of truth who proceeds from the Father—he will testify about me. You also will testify, because you have been with me from the beginning (John 15:26 CSB).

This statement of Jesus Christ says that both the Father and the Son are involved in sending the Holy Spirit. This appears to be the best way of understanding this question—both the Father and the Son send the Holy Spirit.

THIS WAS THE CAUSE FOR THE CHURCH SPLIT (FILIOQUE CLAUSE)

This issue, as to whether the Holy Spirit proceeded from the Father, or the Father and the Son, was the reason given for the church to split into East and West.

The original form of the Nicene Creed declared that, "the Holy Spirit proceeded from the Father." The teaching of St. Augustine in the Western and Latin-speaking church sought to emphasize the strict equality of God the Father and God the Son. He taught that the Spirit proceeds also from the Son.

THE CLAUSE WAS ADDED TO THE NICENE CREED

This teaching eventually was added to the Nicene Creed. The result reads: who proceeds from the Father and the Son. The added words being a translation of the Latin word *filioque* which means "and the Son."

The filioque clause was added by the Western Church to make clear that the Son, Jesus, also sent the Holy Spirit. The addition of this clause is Scriptural; for, as we have just seen, the Bible does teach that the Holy Spirit proceeds from both the Father and the Son. It also emphasizes the Deity of Jesus Christ.

Unfortunately, it was this addition to the Creed that was the "official" reason given for the Church to split into East and West in the year 1054. Of course, this was not the only issue that caused the split between East and West, but it was the reason which was highlighted.

THIS DOES NOT MEAN THAT THE HOLY SPIRIT IS INFERIOR IN NATURE

There is an important point that we need to emphasize. The fact that the Holy Spirit was sent by God the Father and God the Son does not imply that He is inferior in nature to them. The three members of the Trinity are equal in nature.

While equal in nature, they have different duties to perform. It is the mission of the Holy Spirit to do the work of God the Son, Jesus Christ, once Jesus left the earth. Thus, the fact that He was sent by the Father and the Son has nothing to do with His character being less than theirs.

IS THERE AN ETERNAL PROCESSION?

There is also the question as to when this procession occurred. Did it only occur after Jesus ascended into heaven? Or has this sending of the Holy Spirit been something that has been going on forever? The eternal procession of the Holy Spirit seems to be taught in the Psalms:

> When you send your Spirit, new life is born to replenish all the living of the earth (Psalm 104:30 NLT).

During the Old Testament period, the Holy Spirit came forth from God the Father. It was not until after Jesus Christ ascended that the Holy Spirit proceeded from God the Son.

IT IS UNDERSTOOD DIFFERENTLY BY THE ORTHODOX CHURCH

The Orthodox Church, however, understood that the procession of the Holy Spirit was not something that is eternal. They believe that it began only at the time God the Son, Jesus Christ, became a human being.

In sum, while this doctrine of the procession of the Holy Spirit is seemingly a matter of relatively little importance, as far as Scripture is concerned, it became a huge issue in the history of the church.

SUMMARY TO QUESTION 17
WHOM DOES THE HOLY SPIRIT PROCEED FROM? (PROCESSION, FILIOQUE CONTROVERSY)

One of the unfortunate episodes in the history of the church is the split between East and West in A.D. 1054. The reason given was a difference of opinion as to whom the Holy Spirit proceeded from. Was it God the Father, as the Eastern Church emphasized, or God the Father and God the Son, as the Western Church claimed?

In one passage, we are told that the Holy Spirit proceeds from God the Father, while another passage emphasizes that it is God the Son who sends the Holy Spirit.

A third passage says that both the Father and Son send the Spirit. This seems to be the best answer to this question.

This does not mean that the Holy Spirit is lesser in character than the other two members of the Trinity. It indicates that He is subordinate in position to God the Father and God the Son. However, while God the Holy Spirit may be subordinate in position, He is not subordinate in character. Each of the three members of the Holy Trinity are co-equal and co-eternal.

It also seems that the Holy Spirit has "eternally" proceeded from the Father and the Son. This has always been His role in the mysterious inner workings of the Trinity.

However, since there is so little direct information on this subject from Scripture, we need to be careful in any conclusions with which we come up with.

QUESTION 18

What Is the "Name" of the Holy Spirit?

In Matthew 28:19, we have what is called the "Great Commission." In it, Jesus Christ commanded His disciples to make other disciples, and then baptize these believers in the "name" of the three members of the Trinity. We read His command as follows:

> Therefore, go and make disciples of all the nations, baptizing them in the name of the Father and the Son and the Holy Spirit (Matthew 28:19 NLT).

What does He mean by the term "name?" Is it similar to modern usage such as, "in the name of the law?" What exactly does this verse teach us?

1. THE HOLY SPIRIT IS A PERSON

First, we learn the Holy Spirit is a distinct Person. He is mentioned on an equal basis with two other Persons—God the Father and God the Son. In addition, these are "divine" Persons with which He is equated. This is another evidence of His Deity.

2. THE WORD "NAME" IS SINGULAR

The Greek word translated as "name" is singular, not plural. Therefore, the command is to baptize believers in the name of God the Father, and in the name of God of the Son, and in the name of God the Holy Spirit —three distinct Persons.

There are other points that need to be emphasized.

"NAME" IS ALMOST ALWAYS USED OF PERSONS IN SCRIPTURE

When the word "name" is used in the New Testament, it is almost always used of a person. The Greek word *onoma*, translated "name," is used over 225 times in the New Testament, and it always refers to a person, except for four verses (Mark 14:32; Luke 1:26; Luke 24:13; Acts 28:7). In these instances, it refers to the name of a place. It is *never* used of some impersonal force.

Therefore, the normal usage of the term "name" for the Holy Spirit implies a person—not some impersonal force.

THE TERM "NAME" STANDS FOR THE POWER AND AUTHORITY OF A PERSON

The word "name" can also stand in Scripture for "the power and authority of." However, it is always a *person* that it stands for the power and authority of—never some impersonal force. It is not possible for some impersonal force to have personal power or authority. This is a crucial point to understand.

THE TERM "NAME" IS NOT USED IN THE MODERN IMPERSONAL SENSE OF THE WORD

Furthermore, in New Testament Greek we do not find the word "name" used in the modern impersonal sense such as, "in the name of the law" or "in the name of my country." The term was not used in this manner in the New Testament. It was only used in the personal sense.

THE GREAT COMMISSION GIVES TESTIMONY TO THE DEITY OF THE HOLY SPIRIT

In sum, the fact that Jesus told His disciples to baptize believers in the "name" of the Father, Son, and Holy Spirit demonstrates that that they are three distinct Persons.

Furthermore, each of these Persons is God, Himself. This is the mystery of the Holy Trinity. There is one God who consists of three distinct Persons—the Father, the Son, and the Holy Spirit.

SUMMARY TO QUESTION 18
WHAT IS THE "NAME" OF THE HOLY SPIRIT?

In what is known as the "Great Commission," Jesus Christ told His disciples to baptize converts in the name of the Father, the Son, and the Holy Spirit. What does this mean?

In Scripture, the word "name" is used as another way of referring to the person. The word "name" is used in the Bible for the "power and authority of," but only in reference to a person. We do not find the term "name" used in the modern impersonal sense of referring to something other than an actual person—such as "in the name of the law."

Thus, the word "name" in this context has to do with the Person of the Holy Spirit. In other words, new believers are to be baptized into the name of three distinct Persons: The Father, the Son, and the Holy Spirit.

Actually, we learn a number of things from this passage.

First, the three members of the Trinity—the Father, Son, and Holy Spirit —are distinct from one another.

Second, each of the three members, though distinct, is God.

This is the mystery of the Trinity. There is only one God who exists but He consists of three distinct Persons—God the Father, God the Son, and God the Holy Spirit.

The fact that the Holy Spirit is mentioned on an equal basis with two other divine Persons, the Father and the Son, is a further indication of His personhood and Deity.

QUESTION 19

Who Are the Seven Spirits?

A number of times in the Book of Revelation there is a reference to the "seven spirits."

THE SEVEN SPIRITS INTRODUCED

In the introduction to the Book of Revelation, we first read of the seven spirits. John wrote:

> John, To the seven churches in the province of Asia: Grace and peace to you from him who is, and who was, and who is to come, and from the seven spirits before his throne (Revelation 1:4 NIV).

Here the greeting comes from the "seven spirits."

JESUS HAS THE SEVEN SPIRITS

In Chapter 3, we again read of the "seven spirits of God." In this instance, we are told that Jesus holds the seven spirits, as well as the seven stars:

> To the angel of the church in Sardis write: These are the words of him who holds the seven spirits of God and the seven stars. I know your deeds; you have a reputation of being alive, but you are dead (Revelation 3:1 NIV).

Therefore, in some sense, Jesus holds these spirits.

THE SEVEN SPIRITS ARE LINKED WITH FIERY TORCHES

Later, it says the spirits are torches. We read the following:

> Flashes of lightning and rumblings and peals of thunder came from the throne. Seven fiery torches were burning before the throne, which are the seven spirits of God (Revelation 4:5 CSB).

In this case, the seven spirits are said to be seven torches.

THE SLAUGHTERED LAMB HAS THESE SPIRITS

Finally, we read of the slaughtered lamb, Jesus Christ, having these spirits:

> Then I saw one like a slaughtered lamb standing in the midst of the throne and the four living creatures and among the elders. He had seven horns and seven eyes, which are the seven spirits of God sent into all the earth (Revelation 5:6 CSB).

These are the various passages in the Book of Revelation which mention the seven spirits of God. Who are they?

In attempting to answer this question it is important that we make a number of observations. We will begin with what we know for certain.

1. THERE IS ONLY ONE HOLY SPIRIT

First, we emphasize that the Bible teaches there is only one Holy Spirit. Paul wrote the following to the Corinthians:

> One and the same Spirit is active in all these, distributing to each person as he wills (1 Corinthians 12:11 CSB).

To this verse many others could be added. The united testimony of Scripture is that there is only one Spirit of God, one Holy Spirit.

2. THEY ARE DIFFERENT MINISTRIES OF THE ONE SPIRIT

Consequently, if the expression "seven spirits" refers to the Holy Spirit, it does not mean that there are seven different spirits, or that the Holy Spirit is somehow divided into seven different parts.

WHAT THEN DO THESE SEVEN SPIRITS REFER TO?

It could refer to the different ways the Spirit of God expresses Himself. Some see an explanation of the seven spirits in the Book of Isaiah. At the beginning of Chapter 11, we read the following:

> And the Spirit of the LORD will rest on him—the Spirit of wisdom and understanding, the Spirit of counsel and might, the Spirit of knowledge and the fear of the LORD (Isaiah 11:2 NLT).

In this passage Isaiah speaks of the Spirit of the Lord, as well as different aspects of His ministry. The Spirit is mentioned in seven different ways in this verse. The Holy Spirit is the Spirit of the Lord. He is also the Spirit of wisdom, understanding, counsel, might, knowledge, and the Spirit of the fear of the Lord.

Therefore, if this interpretation is correct, the "seven spirits" are not different spirits, but may refer to the complex ministry of the One Holy Spirit.

THE VISION OF ZECHARIAH 4 MAY EXPLAIN THIS PHRASE

The best answer may come from Zechariah 4:2-7 where the prophet sees a solid gold lampstand with seven lamps. Zechariah inquired about the meaning of the vision:

> He asked me, "What do you see?" I replied, "I see a solid gold lampstand with a bowl at the top. The lampstand also has seven lamps at the top with seven spouts for each of the lamps. There are also two olive trees beside it, one on the

right of the bowl and the other on its left." Then I asked the angel who was speaking with me, "What are these, my lord?" "Don't you know what they are?" replied the angel who was speaking with me. I said, "No, my lord." So he answered me, "'This is the word of the Lord to Zerubbabel: 'Not by strength or by might, but by my Spirit,' says the Lord of Armies. 'What are you, great mountain? Before Zerubbabel you will become a plain. And he will bring out the capstone accompanied by shouts of: Grace, grace to it!'" (Zechariah 4:2-7 CSB).

The Apostle John, who was familiar with this passage, used it to identify the Holy Spirit. In fact, it is a perfect example of how the Spirit of God works with the seven congregations who are addressed in Revelation Chapters 2 and 3.

While there is only one Holy Spirit, He does not spread Himself out incrementally in the churches, but is always available, in all of His fullness, to all seven congregations at the same time.

If this is the proper understanding of the term, then it is another example of emphasizing the Deity of the Holy Spirit.

4. THE NUMBER SEVEN REFERS TO COMPLETENESS

There is another point that needs to be considered. The number seven in Scripture often refers to completeness.

For example, the creation of the world occurred in six days with God resting upon the seventh. Consequently, Israel was told to work for six days and to rest on the seventh because this was the pattern set by creation. Moses wrote:

> Six days you shall labor and do all your work, but the seventh day is a Sabbath to the LORD your God. On it you shall not do any work, neither you, nor your son or daughter, nor

your manservant or maidservant, nor your animals, nor the alien within your gates. For in six days the LORD made the heavens and the earth, the sea, and all that is in them, but he rested on the seventh day. Therefore the LORD blessed the Sabbath day and made it holy (Exodus 20:9-11 NIV).

Seven days completes the creation and work week. In the same manner, the reference to the seven spirits refers to the completeness of the Person and work of the Holy Spirit—not to the idea that there are seven distinct spirits.

In sum, whatever we conclude about the exact identity of the seven spirits mentioned in the Book of Revelation, we do know that there is only one Holy Spirit.

SUMMARY TO QUESTION 19
WHO ARE THE SEVEN SPIRITS?

In the Book of Revelation, we find a few occasions where the "seven spirits" are mentioned. The identity of these spirits is not explained. Whatever the correct answer may be, we know that there is only One Holy Spirit. Thus, we cannot divide Him into seven parts.

There have been a number of suggestions as to the identity of these seven spirits. They include the following:

The seven Spirits, referred to in the Book of Revelation, may refer to the various ministries of the one Holy Spirit. We find that seven specific features of the Holy Spirit are mentioned in the Book of Isaiah. Therefore, this could be a reference to the varied ministry of the Holy Spirit.

Another possibility is that John was referring to a passage from Zechariah. If so, he is emphasizing that the ministry of the Holy Spirit in each of the seven churches who are addressed in Revelation 2 and 3, is complete. In other words, it is not spread out incrementally in each of these churches.

It is also possible that the number seven is used symbolically for the completeness of the Holy Spirit. The number seven is used with reference to completeness in both the creation account, as well as the work week for humans. God worked six days and then ceased working on the seventh. Humans work six days and rest on the seventh. It is possible the number seven, with respect to the spirits, has this same idea of completeness.

In sum, there are a couple of possible solutions to this question as to the identity of the seven spirits—though we may not know which of them is the correct answer.

QUESTION 20

Is There a Counterfeit Holy Spirit?

The Bible says there is such a person as the devil. He is a counterfeiter and a liar. Thus, whatever things that God does, we usually find the devil attempting to counterfeit. This is certainly the case when it comes to the work of the Holy Spirit.

The Holy Spirit is God, the Third Person of the Holy Trinity. He is the member of the Godhead who does God's work on earth today. Consequently, we should expect His work to be counterfeited. Scripture tells us that it is. We can make the following observations.

1. THERE IS A COUNTERFEIT SPIRIT

The Bible speaks of not only the genuine Spirit of God but also of a counterfeit spirit. The Apostle Paul warned the church at Corinth about such false spirits. He wrote them with the following warnings:

> But now I fear that you will be tricked, just as Eve was tricked by that lying snake. I am afraid that you might stop thinking about Christ in an honest and sincere way. We told you about Jesus, and you received the Holy Spirit and accepted our message. But you let some people tell you about another Jesus. Now you are ready to receive another spirit and accept a different message . . . Anyway, they are no more than false apostles and dishonest workers. They

only pretend to be apostles of Christ. And it is no wonder. Even Satan tries to make himself look like an angel of light (2 Corinthians 11:3,4,13,14 CEV).

From this passage, we find that there are counterfeits to the Person of Jesus Christ, the gospel message of Christ, as well as to the Holy Spirit. They are all counterfeited by the devil.

Therefore, we should be aware that not everyone who uses the words "Christ," "Gospel," or "Holy Spirit," are actually presenting the truth of God. Indeed, oftentimes they are counterfeiting God's truth.

Furthermore, the devil appears as an "angel of light." This means that his counterfeiting of God's work is not always obvious.

Therefore, we need to be discerning when we hear the terms Christ, Gospel, and Holy Spirit.

2. WE MUST TEST THE SPIRITS

This brings us to our next point. We are warned about a counterfeit Holy Spirit. A thing that is counterfeit always is made to look as close as possible to the genuine article. This passage in Second Corinthians lets us know that everything that "claims" to proceed from the Holy Spirit is not necessarily from the Holy Spirit. We must test the spirits.

John wrote something similar:

> Dear friends, do not believe every spirit, but test the spirits to see if they are from God, because many false prophets have gone out into the world . . . We are from God. Anyone who knows God listens to us; anyone who is not from God does not listen to us. This is how we know the Spirit of truth and the spirit of deception (1 John 4:1,6 CSB).

Believers must test all claims which supposedly come from the Holy Spirit—since there are many false prophets in our world.

QUESTION 20

THE FINAL ANTICHRIST WILL PRODUCE LYING WONDERS

The Apostle Paul warned about a future Antichrist that would do "lying wonders." He explained what will happen in this manner:

> This evil man will come to do the work of Satan with counterfeit power and signs and miracles. He will use every kind of wicked deception to fool those who are on their way to destruction because they refuse to believe the truth that would save them (2 Thessalonians 2:9.10 NLT).

Notice that this individual will produce counterfeit "power" as well as counterfeit "signs." Therefore, it is absolutely necessary to "test the spirits."

Paul wrote elsewhere about this need to test everything. He said:

> But test all things. Hold on to what is good (1 Thessalonians 5:21 CSB).

Believers are to test all things. How do we do this? We do it by comparing everything that we observe to the written Word of God. If someone claims to be speaking for God, yet his teaching contradicts God's Word, then that teaching must be rejected. It does not matter if "signs and wonders" are given.

In sum, we must always be aware of the counterfeiting that the devil is constantly doing. The only way we can know what is genuine, and what is not, is by knowing God's Word. It will always be our faithful guide.

SUMMARY TO QUESTION 20
IS THERE A COUNTERFEIT HOLY SPIRIT?

From the Bible, we find that there is such a person as the devil. He is a liar and a deceiver. We also find that he counterfeits the truth of God.

Scripture warns believers that the Person and work of the Holy Spirit can be counterfeited. In fact, this was already happening at the beginning of the Christian era.

Indeed, the Apostle Paul warned that false spirits were already are in the world deceiving people. The Apostle John gave the same warning. He said that we should not believe every spirit because many false prophets were already out in the world.

We are also told that a final Antichrist will come on the scene and will perform deceptive miracles. He will lead many people away from the truth of God.

Consequently, we should not necessarily believe someone when they ascribe some work, or teaching, to the Holy Spirit. Even if signs and wonders are given, we still should not believe them unless their teaching conforms to God's written Word. It is His Word which must test all things.

QUESTION 21
What Symbols Does the Bible Use to Describe the Holy Spirit?

Scripture often uses material symbols to represent and better explain spiritual truths. In fact, the Bible uses a number of symbols to describe the nature, Person and work of God the Holy Spirit. It is important that we know what they are because we can learn much from an examination of them. They include the following:

1. DOVE

The dove is an important symbol of the Holy Spirit. We find that the Holy Spirit came down in the form of a dove upon the Lord Jesus at His baptism. Luke records what took place:

> The Holy Spirit descended on him in bodily form like a dove. And a voice came from heaven: "You are my Son, whom I love; with you I am well pleased" (Luke 3:22 NIV).

The Holy Spirit is not a dove but He came down like a dove. Thus, a dove is a symbol of the Spirit of God.

2. WATER

The Holy Spirit is also symbolized by water. We find Jesus employing this symbolism when He was at a certain feast in the city of Jerusalem. The Bible explains it in this manner:

> On the last and most important day of the festival, Jesus stood up and cried out, "If anyone is thirsty, let him come to me and drink. The one who believes in me, as the Scripture has said, will have streams of living water flow from deep within him." He said this about the Spirit. Those who believed in Jesus were going to receive the Spirit, for the Spirit had not yet been given because Jesus had not yet been glorified (John 7:37-39 CSB).

Water is a main source of physical life. Jesus Christ is our source of spiritual life. Indeed, He claimed that whoever believed in Him would receive the Spirit. In this instance, the Spirit is likened to streams of living water which flow.

3. FIRE

The Holy Spirit is likened to fire. We read the following words from the prophet Isaiah who compares the Spirit of the Lord to fire:

> The Lord will wash away the filth of the women of Zion; he will cleanse the bloodstains from Jerusalem by a spirit of judgment and a spirit of fire (Isaiah 4:4 NIV).

Fire purifies, as does the work of the Spirit. This is why we find that Holy Spirit compared to fire. He does the purifying or refining work of the Lord.

4. WIND OR BREATH

The wind also symbolizes the work of the Holy Spirit. In fact, on the Day of Pentecost, when the Holy Spirit came down and indwelt believers in a special way, we find the wind playing a role in what took place. We read:

> And suddenly there came a sound from heaven, as of a rushing mighty wind, and it filled the whole house where they were sitting (Acts 2:2 NKJV).

The mighty wind symbolizes the mighty work of God's Spirit.

5. CLOTHING

The Holy Spirit is also symbolized by divine clothing. Jesus promised His disciples that they would be "clothed" from power on high:

> I am going to send you what my Father has promised; but stay in the city until you have been clothed with power from on high (Luke 24:49 NIV).

Those who believe in Jesus Christ are clothed with God's Spirit.

6. OIL

Oil is used symbolically of the work of God the Holy Spirit. The kings of Israel were anointed with oil which symbolized the Spirit of the Lord coming upon them. The Bible says:

> So Samuel took the horn of oil and anointed him in the presence of his brothers, and from that day on the Spirit of the LORD came on David in power. Samuel then went to Ramah (1 Samuel 16:13 NIV).

The anointing with oil symbolized the anointing of the Holy Spirit. Oil had a number of functions in the ancient world. In like manner, the Holy Spirit functions in a number of important ways in the lives of believers.

7. THE SEAL OR THE GUARANTEE

The seal, or guarantee, is also used as a symbol of the work of the Holy Spirit. Paul wrote the following to the Ephesians:

> In him you also were sealed with the promised Holy Spirit when you heard the word of truth, the gospel of your salvation, and when you believed. The Holy Spirit is the down

payment of our inheritance, until the redemption of the possession, to the praise of his glory. (Ephesians 1:13,14 CSB).

The Holy Spirit is the guarantee that God's promises will come to pass. In fact, it is called the "down payment."

8. A STILL SMALL VOICE

The Holy Spirit can be that voice of God which speaks to our innermost being. We find this in the biblical account of Elijah:

> The LORD said, "Go out and stand on the mountain in the presence of the LORD, for the LORD is about to pass by." Then a great and powerful wind tore the mountains apart and shattered the rocks before the LORD, but the LORD was not in the wind. After the wind there was an earthquake, but the LORD was not in the earthquake. After the earthquake came a fire, but the LORD was not in the fire. And after the fire came a gentle whisper. When Elijah heard it, he pulled his cloak over his face and went out and stood at the mouth of the cave. Then a voice said to him, "What are you doing here, Elijah?" (1 Kings 19:11-13 NIV).

The Lord often speaks to believers in that small voice by His Holy Spirit.

9. THE NUMBER SEVEN

Seven speaks of completion. When used of the Holy Spirit it symbolizes the Spirit's fullness and perfection. In the Book of Revelation, we read of the "seven spirits:"

> John: To the seven churches in Asia. Grace and peace to you from the one who is, who was, and who is to come, and from the seven spirits before his throne (Revelation 1:4 CSB).

The Holy Spirit is complete in Himself, and His work is always completed. In other words, He always finishes everything that He sets out to do.

10. THE FINGER OF GOD

Jesus referred to the Holy Spirit as the "finger of God." In a parallel passage, Jesus said that He casts out demons by the Holy Spirit. Luke records it this way:

> But if I cast out demons with the finger of God, surely the kingdom of God has come upon you (Luke 11:20 NKJV).

The Holy Spirit is the One who does the work of God.

11. FIRSTFRUITS

The firstfruits were a symbol of the coming harvest. The initial work of the Holy Spirit symbolizes the final salvation and glorification of each believer. Paul gave this analogy in his letter to the Romans:

> Not only so, but we ourselves, who have the firstfruits of the Spirit, groan inwardly as we wait eagerly for our adoption to sonship, the redemption of our bodies (Romans 8:23 NIV).

This is another indication that each believer will receive their glorification. Indeed, they will be like Jesus Christ someday.

Each of these symbols gives us further insight into the work of the Holy Spirit in the lives of believers. It is thus important that we have some type of understanding of them.

SUMMARY TO QUESTION 21
WHAT SYMBOLS DOES THE BIBLE USE TO DESCRIBE THE HOLY SPIRIT?

At times, God teaches His truth through symbols. In fact, there are a number of different symbols that the Bible uses to describe the Person and work of God the Holy Spirit. These include such things as water, a dove, wind or breath, fire, divine clothing, a pledge or guarantee, the number seven, the finger of God, and firstfruits.

An examination of these symbols will begin to give us an idea of how the Holy Spirit works in our lives. This being the case, it is important that study each of them. This will result in a better understanding as to how the Spirit of God is working with believers in Christ.

Indeed, everything recorded in Scripture is there for a reason, and these symbols teach us numerous biblical truths.

QUESTION 22

Why Is the Holy Spirit Compared to a Dove?

When Jesus Christ was baptized in the Jordan River by John the Baptist, the Bible says that the Holy Spirit came upon Him in the form of a dove. We read of this in the Gospel of Luke. The Bible puts it this way:

> And the Holy Spirit descended on him in the form of a dove. And a voice from heaven said, "You are my beloved Son, and I am fully pleased with you" (Luke 3:22 NLT).

All four gospels testify to this event. Consequently, we find the dove used as a symbol of the Holy Spirit. There are a number of reasons as to why the dove was chosen.

1. THE DOVE SYMBOLIZES PEACE AND REST

The dove is a symbol of peace and rest. When Noah wanted to see if the waters of the Flood had subsided, he sent out a dove. The Book of Genesis says:

> Then he sent out a dove to see whether the water on the earth's surface had gone down, but the dove found no resting place for its foot. It returned to him in the ark because water covered the surface of the whole earth. He reached out and brought it into the ark to himself. So Noah waited seven more days and sent out the dove from the ark again. When

the dove came to him at evening, there was a plucked olive leaf in its beak. So Noah knew that the water on the earth's surface had gone down. After he had waited another seven days, he sent out the dove, but it did not return to him again. (Genesis 8:8-12 CSB).

Here the dove was used to symbolize the new world was ready to be re-inhabited. The violent and sinful people had been judged.

The psalmist wrote about how the dove brings rest:

> Oh, how I wish I had wings like a dove; then I would fly away and rest! (Psalm 55:6 NLT).

This further illustrates what the dove meant to the people. It was a bird which could fly away and rest.

The cooing of doves is seen a symbol of peace and tranquility. We read about this in the Song of Solomon:

> Flowers appear on the earth; the season of singing has come, the cooing of doves is heard in our land (Song of Solomon 2:12 NIV).

Again, the cooing of the dove is a sign that a new season has arrived.

These illustrations are in keeping with what Scripture has to say about the Holy Spirit. For one thing, the fruit of the Holy Spirit is peace. Paul wrote to the Galatians:

> But the fruit of the Spirit is . . . peace (Galatians 5:22 KJV).

As the dove is a symbol of peace, the Holy Spirit brings peace to heart of the believer.

2. THE DOVE REPRESENTS LOVE

We also discover that the dove represents love. In the Song of Solomon, the one who is loved is compared to a dove:

I was asleep, but dreaming: The one I love was at the door, knocking and saying, "My darling, my very own, my flawless dove, open the door for me! My head is drenched with evening dew" (Song of Solomon 5:2 CEV).

This gives further evidence of how the dove was viewed. It was a bird which was used to represent love between two people.

This is in keeping with what the Bible says about the Holy Spirit. Paul wrote to the Romans about the love of the Holy Spirit:

> And hope does not put us to shame, because God's love has been poured out into our hearts through the Holy Spirit, who has been given to us (Romans 5:5 NIV).

The love of God is poured out through the Holy Spirit.

Paul again wrote to the Romans about the love of the Spirit. He put it this way:

> I urge you, brothers and sisters, by our Lord Jesus Christ and by the love of the Spirit, to join me in my struggle by praying to God for me (Romans 15:30 NIV).

To the Galatians, Paul said that the fruit of the Holy Spirit is love:

> But the fruit of the Spirit is . . . love (Galatians 5:22 KJV).

Love is one of the results of the work of the Holy Spirit. Thus, the dove, which represented love to the people of ancient Israel, is a fitting analogy for the Holy Spirit.

3. THE DOVE REPRESENTS PURITY AND PERFECTION

Purity and perfection are other characteristics of a dove. Again, we read in Song of Solomon:

> I was asleep, but dreaming: The one I love was at the door, knocking and saying, "My darling, my very own, my flawless

dove, open the door for me! My head is drenched with evening dew" (Song of Solomon 5:2 CEV).

The lover is compared to a flawless dove.

We also read in Song of Solomon of how the dove symbolizes perfection:

> But my dove, my perfect one, is unique, the only daughter of her mother, the favorite of the one who bore her. The maidens saw her and called her blessed; the queens and concubines praised her (Song of Solomon 6:9 NIV).

The Spirit of God is pure and He is perfect.

4. THE DOVE REPRESENTS HUMILITY

The dove is symbolized as one who is humble, not proud. We read of this in the Song of Solomon. It says:

> My dove in the clefts of the rock, in the hiding places on the mountainside, show me your face, let me hear your voice; for your voice is sweet, and your face is lovely (Song of Solomon 2:14 NIV).

The dove does not seem to be a creature who boasts of itself.

In like manner, Isaiah the prophet wrote about the humility of the servant of the Lord—the Messiah:

> Here is my servant, whom I uphold, my chosen one in whom I delight; I will put my Spirit on him and he will bring justice to the nations. He will not shout or cry out, or raise his voice in the streets (Isaiah 42:1,2 NIV).

The Messiah was to be characterized by humility.

This is an accurate representation of the character of the Messiah, Jesus Christ. Indeed, Jesus Himself said:

Take my yoke upon you and learn from me, for I am gentle and humble in heart, and you will find rest for your souls (Matthew 11:29 NIV).

In the same manner, we find that the Holy Spirit exhibits humility. In fact, the Bible says that He does not speak on His own authority, or about Himself, but rather He always speaks about Jesus. Christ said:

> However, when He, the Spirit of truth, has come, He will guide you into all truth; for He will not speak on His own authority, but whatever He hears He will speak; and He will tell you things to come (John 16:13 NKJV).

The Contemporary English Version puts it this way:

> The Spirit shows what is true and will come and guide you into the full truth. The Spirit doesn't speak on his own. He will tell you only what he has heard from me, and he will let you know what is going to happen (John 16:13 CEV).

The ministry of the Holy Spirit is to further the ministry of Jesus.

5. THE DOVE IS HARMLESS

The dove is also considered to be a harmless bird. Jesus illustrated this truth when He spoke about how His disciples were to behave. We read:

> I am sending you out like sheep among wolves. Therefore be as shrewd as snakes and as innocent as doves (Matthew 10:16 NIV).

The dove is seen to be an innocent bird.

The Bible says that the Holy Spirit can be grieved but never says that He can be angered:

> And do not grieve the Holy Spirit of God, with whom you were sealed for the day of redemption (Ephesians 4:30 NIV).

The Holy Spirit has been given to help believers—not to harm them.

6. THE DOVE UNDERSTANDS THE CHANGE OF THE SEASONS

The dove also understands when the seasons change. The prophet Jeremiah noted:

> Even the stork in the sky knows her appointed seasons, and the dove, the swift and the thrush observe the time of their migration. But my people do not know the requirements of the LORD (Jeremiah 8:7 NIV).

The dove is aware of what is taking place.

In Song of Solomon, we read:

> Flowers appear on the earth; the season of singing has come, the cooing of doves is heard in our land (Song of Solomon 2:12 NIV).

In the same manner, the Holy Spirit, as God, knows all things. Indeed, He is aware of everything which is taking place on the earth.

7. THE DOVE IS A CLEAN BIRD

Since the dove was used for sacrifice, it is a ceremonially "clean" animal. We read of the offering of the dove in Leviticus:

> And when the days of her purifying are completed, whether for a son or for a daughter, she shall bring to the priest at the entrance of the tent of meeting a lamb a year old for a burnt offering, and a pigeon or a turtledove for a sin offering (Leviticus 12:6 ESV).

This is another example of the purity of the Holy Spirit.

Therefore, from a search of the Scripture, we find that the comparison of the Holy Spirit to a dove has a number of different meanings.

SUMMARY TO QUESTION 22
WHY IS THE HOLY SPIRIT COMPARED TO A DOVE?

God chose the symbol of the dove to represent the Holy Spirit. As we search the Scripture, we discover that the dove represented a number of things to the people in the ancient world.

We find that the dove was a peace symbol. The Spirit of God brings peace and rest to the hearts of those who know Jesus Christ as their Savior.

The Bible says that the dove also was a symbol of love. One of the fruits of the Holy Spirit is the love that He produces in the life of the believer.

The dove was representative of purity and perfection. This is an apt description of the Spirit of God. He is pure and perfect in all of His ways.

We also find that the dove was viewed as a harmless bird. The Holy Spirit gently works in the hearts and lives of those who have trusted Christ.

Seemingly the dove represented humility to the people. This certainly fits with how the Bible describes the Holy Spirit. Indeed, He does not speak about Himself but rather speaks only of God the Son, Jesus Christ.

Scripture says the dove also understands when the seasons change. The Holy Spirit, as God, understands all things. Nothing escapes His knowledge.

A dove is a clean bird that can be used for sacrifice. In the same manner, the Holy Spirit has no faults or blemishes whatsoever. As God, the Holy Spirit is perfect in character.

Consequently, the dove is an appropriate symbol for the Holy Spirit.

QUESTION 23

Why Is the Holy Spirit Compared to Water?

In the ancient world water was a precious commodity. The lack of rain in certain areas made the catching and saving of rainwater something which was of the utmost importance.

In Scripture, we find water is used as a symbol of the Spirit of God. The following are examples of this use:

1. WATER SYMBOLIZES THE RECEPTION OF THE HOLY SPIRIT

Water signifies the reception of the Holy Spirit. The prophet Ezekiel compared the Spirit of God with the cleansing of the heart:

> I will sprinkle clean water on you, and you will be clean; I will cleanse you from all your impurities and from all your idols. I will give you a new heart and put a new spirit in you; I will remove from you your heart of stone and give you a heart of flesh. And I will put my Spirit in you and move you to follow my decrees and be careful to keep my laws (Ezekiel 36:25-27 NIV).

Water is seen as symbol of the Spirit of God coming into a person's life and cleansing their heart from sin.

2. THE POURING OF WATER AT THE FEAST OF TABERNACLES

At the Feast of Tabernacles, or Booths, the priest would pour water next to the altar as the final ritual of this feast. This event looked forward to the time the Messiah would come.

The prophet Zechariah wrote of that great day when Messiah, the King, would arrive:

> Then the survivors from all the nations that have attacked Jerusalem will go up year after year to worship the King, the LORD Almighty, and to celebrate the Feast of Tabernacles (Zechariah 14:16 NIV).

Thus, the water symbolized the day of the Messiah, the King.

We find this same truth taught in the New Testament. It is in this context, at the Festival of Tabernacles or Booths, that Jesus spoke of "living water." We read of the following event in the life of Christ:

> On the last and most important day of the festival, Jesus stood up and shouted, "If you are thirsty, come to me and drink! Have faith in me, and you will have life-giving water flowing from deep inside you, just as the Scriptures say." Jesus was talking about the Holy Spirit, who would be given to everyone that had faith in him. The Spirit had not yet been given to anyone, since Jesus had not yet been given his full glory (John 7:37-39 CEV).

Jesus claimed to be the fulfillment of the Messianic hope of the people. The Holy Spirit would be the evidence in the lives of believers that His claims were true. Out of their innermost being would come rivers, or torrents, of living or life-giving water. This was Jesus' prediction of the coming of the Holy Spirit.

3. JESUS GIVES LIFE-GIVING WATER TO THOSE WHO BELIEVE

Jesus told a woman in Samaria that He is the One who gives living water to those who have a spiritual thirst. We read:

But those who drink the water I give them will never thirst. Indeed, the water I give them will become in them a spring of water welling up to eternal life (John 4:14 NIV).

In this context, water is a symbol of the Holy Spirit that represents eternal life.

4. THE LORD GIVES THE WATER OF LIFE

The Bible also speaks of the Lord giving the water of life:

> He said to me: "It is done. I am the Alpha and the Omega, the Beginning and the End. To the thirsty I will give water without cost from the spring of the water of life (Revelation 21:6 NIV).

This water brings life to those who drink it.

John also wrote:

> The Spirit and the bride say, "Come!" Everyone who hears this should say, "Come!" If you are thirsty, come! If you want life-giving water, come and take it. It's free! (Revelation 22:17 CEV).

Jesus offers the water of life. Again, the Holy Spirit represents that life-giving water that quenches our spiritual thirst.

5. WATER IS SYMBOLIC OF SATISFACTION AND PROSPERITY

In the Bible, we find that water signifies such things as satisfaction and prosperity. The psalmist wrote:

> May his reign be as refreshing as the springtime rains—like the showers that water the earth (Psalm 72:6 NLT).

Since the rains were absolutely necessary for the survival of those people, they represented prosperity and satisfaction. Indeed, without the rains the people would have neither.

In the same manner, without the Spirit of God none of us can have spiritual satisfaction.

Isaiah the prophet records the Lord predicting that He will bring water to the barren places of the desert:

> I will make rivers flow on barren heights, and springs within the valleys. I will turn the desert into pools of water, and the parched ground into springs (Isaiah 41:18 NIV).

This again testifies to the value of water. The Lord also said:

> I am creating something new. There it is! Do you see it? I have put roads in deserts, streams in thirsty lands (Isaiah 43:19 CEV).

Water is thus a fitting symbol for the Person and work of the Holy Spirit. For only with Him, can an individual achieve satisfaction and prosperity in this life.

Therefore, from Scripture we find that water has a number of important symbolic meanings for the believer. Indeed, it is a wonderful symbol of the work of the Spirit of God in the lives of His people.

SUMMARY TO QUESTION 23
WHY IS THE HOLY SPIRIT COMPARED TO WATER?

In the dry and desert world of the Bible, water was an extremely important commodity. Consequently, we find that the Bible uses water as a symbol of the Holy Spirit. We note that there are a number of essential truths we learn from this comparison.

In the Book of Ezekiel, water symbolizes the reception of the Holy Spirit. It represents the cleansing which takes place when a person puts their trust in the God of Scripture.

We find the same thing in the New Testament. Jesus said that He would give life-giving water to those who have believed in Him. This was referring to the Holy Spirit. In fact, the reception of the Holy Spirit would be the evidence that a person had truly believed in the Lord.

The Bible also uses water as a symbol of satisfaction and prosperity. This fits well with the Holy Spirit who satisfies and prospers those who believe in the Lord. Indeed, spiritual prosperity is impossible without the work of the Holy Spirit in the life of the person. On the other hand, when the Holy Spirit is leading and guiding someone, they will truly prosper.

In sum, water is a fitting symbol of the work of the Holy Spirit. Only the God of the Bible can solve the problem of our spiritual thirst.

QUESTION 24

Why Is the Holy Spirit Compared to Fire?

The Bible uses many different symbols for the Holy Spirit. One of them is fire. We find John the Baptist comparing the Holy Spirit to fire:

> I baptize you with water for repentance, but he who is coming after me is mightier than I, whose sandals I am not worthy to carry. He will baptize you with the Holy Spirit and fire (Matthew 3:11 ESV).

John said that the Holy Spirit will baptize people with the Holy Spirit and with fire. Consequently, we have this comparison of the Spirit of God with fire.

FIRE APPEARED ON THE DAY OF PENTECOST

On the Day of Pentecost, we are told that "tongues like fire" appeared on the disciples when the Holy Spirit came down in a special way. The Book of Acts records it as follows:

> Then they saw what looked like fiery tongues moving in all directions, and a tongue came and settled on each person there. The Holy Spirit took control of everyone, and they began speaking whatever languages the Spirit let them speak (Acts 2:3,4 CEV).

Among other things, this would remind the Jews of God speaking to Moses by means of the burning bush. Scripture records what occurred as follows:

> There the angel of the LORD appeared to him in flames of fire from within a bush. Moses saw that though the bush was on fire it did not burn up (Exodus 3:2 NIV).

This was a well-known miracle for all of the children of Israel.

FIRE SPEAKS OF GOD'S PRESENCE AND POWER

Fire speaks symbolically of God's presence and His power. It also testifies to His approval of what is occurring.

For example, God's power and approval was demonstrated through the fire that came down and consumed the burnt offering that Elijah the prophet had prepared. The Bible explains what took place in this manner:

> Then the fire of the Lord fell and burned up the sacrifice, the wood, the stones and the soil, and also licked up the water in the trench (1 Kings 18:38 NIV).

The fire of the Lord came down and consumed the sacrifice. This is how God demonstrated His presence and power in a practical way.

GOD HIMSELF IS COMPARED TO FIRE

We also find that the God of the Bible is compared to fire. The writer to the Hebrews put it this way:

> For our God is a consuming fire (Hebrews 12:29 KJV).

Since the Holy Spirit is God, it is not surprising that He also is compared with fire.

FIRE CAN SPEAK OF THE PURGING OF SIN

Fire is used as symbolizing God purging sin. In the Book of Malachi, we read about this:

> The Lord will purify the descendants of Levi, as though they were gold or silver. Then they will bring the proper offerings to the Lord (Malachi 3:3 CEV).

Here we find that sin is purified by fire.

Isaiah the prophet wrote of something similar when he spoke of the "spirit of burning." He explained it in this manner:

> The Lord has washed away the filth of the daughters of Zion and cleansed the bloodguilt from the heart of Jerusalem by a spirit of judgment and a spirit of burning (Isaiah 4:4 CSB).

Thus, the Lord uses fire to purge sin.

After Isaiah saw the Lord upon His throne, He had to be purged from his sin with fire. We read the following:

> Then one of the seraphs flew to me with a live coal in his hand, which he had taken with tongs from the altar. With it he touched my mouth and said, "See, this has touched your lips; your guilt is taken away and your sin atoned for" (Isaiah 6:6,7 NIV).

Sin is purged through fire.

FIRE SPEAKS OF GOD'S JUDGMENT

Fire can also speak of God's judgment. We read of this in the Book of Leviticus:

> So fire came out from the presence of the LORD and consumed them, and they died before the LORD (Leviticus 10:2 NIV).

Those who rejected the message of Jesus will be judged by means of fire. The city of Jerusalem, with its temple, was destroyed by fire one generation after the coming of the Holy Spirit.

The ultimate destination for unbelievers is the "lake of fire." Therefore, fire speaks of God's judgment and is a proper symbol of the work of the Holy Spirit.

SUMMARY TO QUESTION 24
WHY IS THE HOLY SPIRIT COMPARED TO FIRE?

Fire is used symbolically in Scripture in a number of ways. Among them, we find that the person and work of the Holy Spirit is compared to fire. Indeed, it tells us a number of things about who He is, as well as what He does.

For one thing, God's presence and His approval are symbolized by fire. In fact, the Lord used fire to demonstrate that Elijah was a genuine prophet of God. He did this by sending fire from heaven and consuming the sacrifice which Elijah put on the altar.

God Himself is compared to fire. The Bible says that He is a "consuming fire."

Fire is also symbolic of God purging sins from believers. We are told that He cleanses believers through the refining process.

Fire is representative of judging unbelief. Scripture says that there will be a final judgment where unbelievers will be thrown into the lake of fire. Sadly, fire will be their punishment for all eternity because of their rejection of the work of the Holy Spirit who reveals Jesus Christ to them.

Thus, fire is a fitting symbol for the Spirit of God.

QUESTION 25

Why Is the Holy Spirit Compared to the Wind?

The work of the Holy Spirit is compared to the wind. Jesus Himself made this comparison when He was speaking to the religious leader Nicodemus. John records Him saying the following:

> Just as you can hear the wind but can't tell where it comes from or where it is going, so you can't explain how people are born of the Spirit (John 3:8 NLT).

In this instance, God's Spirit is compared with the wind. What do the Spirit of God and the wind have in common? Why the comparison?

WIND IS AN OBVIOUS COMPARISON

Wind would seem to be the most obvious comparison to the Holy Spirit. The same word in both Hebrew and Greek can mean either "wind," "spirit," or "breath" depending upon the context. Wind, or breath, speaks of life.

In the Book of Ezekiel, we read about the bones of a body coming together without any breath or life in them. Then the Lord causes the four winds to breathe life into the dead body. We read about it in this manner:

> So I spoke these words, just as he told me. Suddenly as I spoke, there was a rattling noise all across the valley. The

bones of each body came together and attached themselves as they had been before. Then as I watched, muscles and flesh formed over the bones. Then skin formed to cover their bodies, but they still had no breath in them. Then he said to me, "Speak to the winds and say: 'This is what the Sovereign LORD says: Come, O breath, from the four winds! Breathe into these dead bodies so that they may live again.'" So I spoke as he commanded me, and the wind entered the bodies, and they began to breathe. They all came to life and stood up on their feet—a great army of them (Ezekiel 37:7-10 NLT).

Here the four winds bring about the "breath of life" in these dead bodies. As we indicated, the same word is used for both wind and breath. Consequently, we have a natural comparison between the two.

THE CHARACTERISTICS OF WIND

Indeed, the characteristics of wind make an excellent comparison to the work of the Holy Spirit in a number of different ways. We can cite the following:

1. THE WIND IS INVISIBLE

Wind is invisible. One cannot see the wind. In the same way, God's Spirit is invisible. God, by nature, is spirit. Jesus made this clear:

God is Spirit, and those who worship Him must worship in spirit and truth (John 4:24 NKJV).

God's form is not physical like ours. He is spirit.

We find that Jesus emphasized that a spirit or ghost has no physical form. On the day of His resurrection, when the Lord appeared to His disciples in the upper room, He said the following to them:

Look at my hands and my feet. It is I myself! Touch me and see; a ghost does not have flesh and bones, as you see I have (Luke 24:39 NIV).

A spirit, or a ghost, does not have a physical form. It is invisible.

Like the wind, the invisible Holy Spirit works in ways which are unseen to the human eye.

2. THE RESULTS CAN BE SEEN AND FELT

Although one cannot see the wind, the results can be seen and felt. The same is true of the Holy Spirit. Although He cannot be seen, the results of His work can be seen and felt.

On the Day of Pentecost, we read of this. The Bible says:

> On the day of Pentecost, seven weeks after Jesus' resurrection, the believers were meeting together in one place. Suddenly, there was a sound from heaven like the roaring of a mighty windstorm in the skies above them, and it filled the house where they were meeting (Acts 2:1,2 NLT).

Here we find the coming of the Holy Spirit represented by a mighty windstorm. This illustrates that humans are able to feel the wind and view its results.

3. THE WIND IS POWERFUL

Wind can be very powerful. Humankind is used to seeing devastating things happen when wind is whipped up in a powerful way.

In the same manner, the work of the Holy Spirit is powerful. The Bible says that He was involved in creating the heavens and the earth:

> The earth was barren, with no form of life; it was under a roaring ocean covered with darkness. But the Spirit of God was moving over the water (Genesis 1:2 CEV).

The wind can be powerful and the Holy Spirit is certainly powerful!

4. THE WIND IS UNEXPLAINABLE

Wind cannot be explained. We do not understand where it comes from or where it goes. Likewise, the work of the Holy Spirit, who is God, cannot be explained. Jesus compared it to the wind:

> The wind blows where it wishes, and you hear the sound of it, but cannot tell where it comes from and where it goes. So is everyone who is born of the Spirit (John 3:8 NKJV).

Who can explain the wind? Who can explain the work of God? The answer, of course, is nobody.

5. THE WIND GOES WHERE IT WISHES

Wind goes where it desires. It does not go where someone guides it. In the same way, the Holy Spirit of God does what He wills. Paul wrote to the Corinthians:

> But one and the same Spirit works all these things, distributing to each one individually as He wills (1 Corinthians 12:11 NKJV).

Each of these symbols of the wind serve to highlight various aspects of the work of God the Holy Spirit.

HE IS GOD'S MIGHTY WIND IN THE OLD TESTAMENT

There is something else which we must note. In the Hebrew Old Testament, the word translated "spirit" is *ruach*. In certain contexts, the word can be translated as "wind," while at other times the word is translated "spirit." The context must decide.

At times, it is used for a fresh breeze that would blow at the end of a very hot day. However, the common meaning of the term is a hot, fierce, gusty, and devastating wind.

The word can also mean "breath"—but not the normal breath of human beings. There is another Hebrew word used for this.

When it is translated as "breath," it has the idea of someone in passion or violently exerting himself in heavy breathing.

Therefore, God's Spirit can be described as God's stormy wind, or God's fierce breathing. This gives us further insight into the character and work of God's Holy Spirit.

SUMMARY TO QUESTION 25
WHY IS THE HOLY SPIRIT COMPARED TO THE WIND?

The Holy Spirit is compared to many things, including the wind. In fact, we find that the same words in Hebrew and Greek can be translated by either "spirit" or "wind." The comparison with wind is quite appropriate for a number of reasons:

For one thing, the wind is invisible. We know that it is there, but we cannot see it. The same can be said of the work of the Spirit of God. We know that He is working, but we do not see Him.

Though the wind is invisible, its results can be seen and felt. In the same manner, when the Holy Spirit works in our lives, the results can be seen and felt.

The wind can also be very powerful. Each of us has seen what can happen when a powerful wind whips up. In the same manner, when the Holy Spirit works His powerful will in the lives of people, then we too can view the results.

The wind is unexplainable. We do not know where it comes from or where it is going. Likewise, the Spirit of God works in unexplainable ways. Where and how He is going to work His divine will is a mystery to us.

Finally, the wind blows where it wishes. Nobody can guide its direction. The same is true of the Spirit of God. He works in His unique way and there is nobody, in heaven or on earth, who can tell Him what to do.

In sum, the comparison of the Spirit of God to wind teaches us a number of valuable lessons.

QUESTION 26

Why Is the Holy Spirit Compared to Clothing?

After Jesus Christ rose from the dead He told His disciples to remain in Jerusalem until God clothed, or dressed, them with power from on high. We read about this in the Gospel of Luke where it says the following:

> I am going to send you what my Father has promised; but stay in the city until you have been clothed with power from on high (Luke 24:49 NIV).

In this context, the work of the Holy Spirit is compared to clothing. Jesus promised that the Holy Spirit would clothe, with power, those who believed in Him.

The idea is that *God* would clothe the believers with power—not that they would clothe themselves. Consequently, the emphasis is what God does for the believer—it is not anything that the believer can do.

THE POWER OF THE HOLY SPIRIT COMES FROM GOD

The Bible emphasizes that the power of the Holy Spirit, which comes from God, alone, allows believers to testify about Jesus Christ. Jesus Himself said:

> But you will receive power when the Holy Spirit comes on you; and you will be my witnesses in Jerusalem, and in all

Judea and Samaria, and to the ends of the earth (Acts 1:8 NIV).

This power is available to every believer the moment they trust Christ as their Savior. They are now in a position to tell everyone about the risen Lord.

CLOTHING IS USED ELSEWHERE IN SCRIPTURE TO REVEAL SPIRITUAL TRUTH

We find a number of illustrations in the Bible where clothing is used to reveal spiritual truth. They include the following examples:

WE ARE TO CLOTHE OURSELVES WITH HIS ATTRIBUTES

For one thing, we find that God's people are to clothe themselves with the attributes of the Lord Himself. Paul wrote the following to the Colossians:

> Therefore, as God's chosen people, holy and dearly loved, clothe yourselves with compassion, kindness, humility, gentleness and patience (Colossians 3:12 NIV).

There are a number of attributes of God with which believers are commanded to clothe themselves with. In other words, like physical clothing, we are to make these attributes part of our person which completely covers us.

OUR SPIRITUAL CLOTHING IS COMPARED TO ARMOR

Paul told the Thessalonians that we are to clothe ourselves with faith and love—in the same manner in which a solider will put on armor:

> But since we belong to the day, let us be sober, putting on faith and love as a breastplate, and the hope of salvation as a helmet (First Thessalonians 5:8 NIV).

The armor of God is the clothing of the Christian.

THE BRIDE OF CHRIST RETURNS WITH PURE CLOTHING

The Bride of Christ is to wear fine clothing when she returns with Christ. We read about this in the Book of Revelation:

> Fine linen, bright and clean, was given her to wear." (Fine linen stands for the righteous acts of God's holy people.) (Revelation 19:8 NIV).

The bride will be dressed for the wedding. Jesus is the groom.

In sum, clothing in Scripture can mean more than mere material clothing.

SUMMARY TO QUESTION 26
WHY IS THE HOLY SPIRIT COMPARED TO CLOTHING?

The illustration of God clothing believers with the Holy Spirit emphasizes an important truth. The Holy Spirit completely covers those who have trusted Christ.

This is something the Spirit does by Himself—the believer has nothing to do with it. We do not clothe ourselves with the Holy Spirit—He clothes us.

Furthermore, God clothes us with His power to become a witness for Him. Indeed, we are given the power of the Holy Spirit to testify of Jesus Christ. He clothes us to accomplish this task.

Yet there are times that we are told to clothe ourselves with certain attributes or characteristics of God. In fact, we are commanded to "put on" these attributes—to be Christ-like in our behavior.

Again, we can only accomplish this through the power of the Holy Spirit.

Clothing is thus used as a figure of speech in Scripture to reveal vital spiritual truth.

QUESTION 27

Why Is the Holy Spirit Compared to a Pledge or a Guarantee?

One of the comparisons of the Holy Spirit is to a "guarantee." We find this used by the Apostle Paul when he wrote to the Ephesians. It says:

> In him you also, when you heard the word of truth, the gospel of your salvation, and believed in him, were sealed with the promised Holy Spirit, who is the guarantee of our inheritance until we acquire possession of it, to the praise of his glory (Ephesians 1:13,14 ESV).

The Holy Spirit makes us certain that God will give us what He promised. He guarantees that we will receive our inheritance.

Paul told the Corinthians the Holy Spirit is a down payment of what is to come. He wrote the following words in his second letter to that church:

> He has also put his seal on us and given us the Spirit in our hearts as a down payment (2 Corinthians 1:22 CSB).

Paul emphasized this again later in his second letter to the Corinthians. He said:

> Now the one who prepared us for this very purpose is God, who gave us the Spirit as a down payment (2 Corinthians 5:5 CSB).

The Holy Spirit is our down payment that more is to come.

WHAT WE LEARN FROM THE COMPARISON

There are a number of things that we can learn from this comparison of the Holy Spirit with a deposit, or a pledge.

1. IT REFERS TO AN OBLIGATION TO PAY

The Holy Spirit is the deposit, or pledge, for the believer. The Greek word *arrabon* means the first installment, down payment, or deposit. The idea is that it pays part of the purchase price ahead of time to make an agreement or contract valid. It is a guarantee that the remainder will eventually be paid. The down payment represents an obligation on the part of the one who makes the deposit.

2. THE HOLY SPIRIT IS THE DOWN PAYMENT

The Holy Spirit, therefore, is the down payment from God. This obligates God to follow through with what He has pledged. The fulfillment of all God's promises toward those who believe is now guaranteed. It symbolizes the fact that believers are secure in Jesus Christ because He has promised to keep His part of the agreement. Paul wrote elsewhere:

> Not only so, but we ourselves, who have the firstfruits of the Spirit, groan inwardly as we wait eagerly for our adoption to sonship, the redemption of our bodies (Romans 8:23 NIV).

The Holy Spirit gives us a foretaste of the glory that is to come. The Contemporary English Version says:

> The Spirit makes us sure about what we will be in the future. But now we groan silently, while we wait for God to show that we are his children. This means that our bodies will also be set free (Romans 8:23 CEV).

God always keeps His promises. There is certainly no question of this.

3. THIS EMPHASIZES THAT GOD ALWAYS KEEPS HIS WORD

All of this emphasizes the fact that God keeps His Word. When He promises something, He will come through with His promises. The psalmist wrote:

> And the words of the Lord are flawless, like silver purified in a crucible, like gold refined seven times (Psalm 12:6 NIV).

The Lord means what He says, and He says what He means. His promises are certain.

4. HE GUARANTEES THE FUTURE INHERITANCE OF BELIEVERS

The Holy Spirit is the down payment, or deposit, that God will keep His Word and give us the promised blessings that are found in Scripture. This includes the future inheritance that the believer is promised.

One of these promises is that believers are joint-heirs, or co-heirs, with Jesus Christ. Paul wrote to the Romans:

> The Spirit Himself bears witness with our spirit that we are children of God, and if children, then heirs—heirs of God and joint heirs with Christ, if indeed we suffer with Him, that we may also be glorified together (Romans 8:16,17 NKJV).

We are promised that we will share in His eternal glory. Certain things which belong to Him will also belong to us. The Holy Spirit confirms this wonderful truth in the heart of the believer.

The fulfillment of this promise will take place when Jesus Christ comes back to earth to dwell with believers. The Bible promises this will indeed happen one day.

John wrote the following in the Book of Revelation:

> I heard a loud shout from the throne, saying, "Look, the home of God is now among his people! He will live with

them, and they will be his people. God himself will be with them. He will remove all of their sorrows, and there will be no more death or sorrow or crying or pain. For the old world and its evils are gone forever" (Revelation 21:3,4 NLT).

God has promised a wonderful future for those who believe. The Holy Spirit is the One who guarantees this. Therefore, we can have complete assurance that it will indeed come to pass.

SUMMARY TO QUESTION 27
WHY IS THE HOLY SPIRIT COMPARED TO A PLEDGE OR GUARANTEE?

The Spirit of God is compared to something which is pledged or guaranteed. Indeed, we are told that the Holy Spirit is given to each believer as a pledge, or deposit, that God will keep the agreement that He has made with those who trust Christ. The Spirit is the down payment that assures us that God will keep His part of the bargain.

This includes all of the promised blessings that are to come. The Bible has so many wonderful things in store for those who believe in Jesus.

Among other things, the Holy Spirit confirms that we are co-heirs, or joint-heirs, with Jesus Christ. Many of the things which rightly belong to Him will also belong to us. This is because we are "in Christ." The Spirit of God confirms this to our hearts.

In sum, God has given us His Holy Spirit as a guarantee that He will come through with all of His promises toward us.

QUESTION 28

Why Is the Holy Spirit Associated with the Anointing of Oil?

The Holy Spirit is associated with the anointing of oil. What does this mean? Why the connection between anointing with oil and the work of the Holy Spirit?

THE ANOINTING WITH OIL REPRESENTS THE COMING OF THE SPIRIT

In the Old Testament, we find that the anointing with oil was representative of the coming of the Holy Spirit upon a person. For instance, the prophet Samuel used oil to anoint David as king of Israel. We are told the following:

> Then Samuel took the horn of oil and anointed him in the midst of his brothers; and the Spirit of the LORD came upon David from that day forward. So Samuel arose and went to Ramah (1 Samuel 16:13 NKJV).

When David was anointed with oil, the Bible says that the Holy Spirit came upon him. Therefore, we find oil symbolizing the work of the Holy Spirit.

THE ANOINTING SIGNIFIES DIFFERENT THINGS

The anointing with oil is used in Scripture to signify a number of important things. They include the following:

1. THE MESSIAH IS THE ANOINTED ONE

The Hebrew term translated "Messiah," as well as the Greek term "Christ," means "the anointed one." The fact that the Holy Spirit is compared to the "anointing with oil" associates Him with the Messiah. The Bible says that Jesus, the Messiah, was anointed with the Holy Spirit.

The Book of Acts records Peter saying:

> How God anointed Jesus of Nazareth with the Holy Spirit and power, and how he went around doing good and healing all who were under the power of the devil, because God was with him (Acts 10:38 NIV).

It was God the Father who anointed Jesus Christ with the Holy Spirit for the work of the ministry.

2. THE ANOINTING REFERS TO POWER FOR THE WORK OF THE MINISTRY

Power for ministry is also associated with the anointing with oil. Isaiah the prophet wrote about this when he predicted the coming of the Messiah. He put it this way:

> The Spirit of the Sovereign LORD is on me, because the LORD has anointed me to proclaim good news to the poor. He has sent me to bind up the brokenhearted, to proclaim freedom for the captives and release from darkness for the prisoners (Isaiah 61:1 NIV).

Here the prophet says that the Spirit of God has anointed this person for the work of the ministry.

In this instance, the prophecy was fulfilled by Jesus Christ. Indeed, after Jesus read this passage in a synagogue in Nazareth, Luke records the following took place:

Then he rolled up the scroll, gave it back to the attendant and sat down. The eyes of everyone in the synagogue were fastened on him. He began by saying to them, Today this scripture is fulfilled in your hearing" (Luke 4:20-21 NIV).

According to Jesus, His coming to the earth fulfilled the prediction of the Lord anointing His servant to proclaim the good news. Though Jesus fulfilled this prophecy at His First Coming, it did not consist of a literal anointing with oil. Thus, the oil spoke of the power to do the work of the ministry.

3. OIL AND HEALING ARE ASSOCIATED TOGETHER

Healing of the body is often associated with anointing with oil. We read in Isaiah:

> From your head to your toes there isn't a healthy spot. Bruises, cuts, and open sores go without care or oil to ease the pain (Isaiah 1:6 CEV).

In this context, oil is seen as a healing agent.

James also wrote about the use of oil in a healing context:

> Is anyone among you sick? He should call for the elders of the church, and they are to pray over him, anointing him with oil in the name of the Lord (James 5:14 CSB).

The anointing is literal in these instances. On certain occasions, actual oil was put upon the person for healing. However, there is some question as to whether the oil itself was supposed to heal, or whether it was symbolic of God's healing touch through the Holy Spirit.

4. THE ANOINTING OF THE HOLY SPIRIT HELPS BELIEVERS UNDERSTAND GOD'S TRUTH

Finally, we are told that believers in Christ have an anointing from the Spirit to understand God's truth. John wrote:

Christ, the Holy One, has blessed you, and now all of you understand (1 John 2:20 CEV).

We can understand the truth of God because the Holy Spirit has anointed our hearts and minds to His truth. In other words, He has opened up our hearts to the truth.

John also emphasized how the Holy Spirit always teaches the truth. He is the only infallible source for truth about Jesus Christ. We read:

> But Christ has blessed you with the Holy Spirit. Now the Spirit stays in you, and you don't need any teachers. The Spirit is truthful and teaches you everything. So stay one in your heart with Christ, just as the Spirit has taught you to do (1 John 2: 27 CEV).

It is important that the Holy Spirit teaches the believers truth—for He is the only One who can assure us that we do indeed have the truth.

In sum, anointing with oil has a number of important lessons for us when it is associated with the work of the Holy Spirit. This being the case, we should pay close attention to these passages which use this analogy.

SUMMARY TO QUESTION 28
WHY IS THE HOLY SPIRIT ASSOCIATED WITH THE ANOINTING OF OIL?

In the Bible, we find the Holy Spirit associated with anointing someone with oil. This has a number of meanings.

For one thing, the kings of Israel were anointed with oil. This represented the initial coming of the Holy Spirit in their lives. The idea is that they were to rule the nation through the power of God's Spirit rather than with their own power.

Elsewhere we find the anointing is associated in Scripture with power to do the ministry. Jesus Christ, as the promised Messiah, was anointed with the Holy Spirit to do God's special work. In fact, when Jesus read a passage, which spoke of the anointing of the Messiah, He said that this particular passage spoke of Him! He was the "Anointed One."\

In some places, we find that physical healing is associated with the anointing of oil. Oil was put on the person for healing purposes. At times, the oil itself was seen as the healing agent while at other times it was representative of the work of the Holy Spirit.

Anointing of oil also speaks of the understanding of the truth of God. The Apostle John wrote about the anointing which all believers have received so that they can be able to know God's truth. This is through the work of the Holy Spirit in our lives.

Oil, is therefore, an appropriate symbol for God's Spirit since it is the Holy Spirit who performs the work of the ministry through believers. He also heals those who are sick, and gives understanding to God's truth to those who wish to hear it.

QUESTION 29

Why Is the Seal, or Insignia, a Symbol of God's Spirit?

A seal, or insignia, is a mark of ownership. The Bible says that the Holy Spirit is God's mark of ownership of the believer. Paul wrote to the Ephesians:

> And you also were included in Christ when you heard the word of truth, the gospel of your salvation. When you believed, you were marked in him with a seal, the promised Holy Spirit, who is a deposit guaranteeing our inheritance until the redemption of those who are God's possession—to the praise of his glory (Ephesians 1:13,14 NIV).

In this passage, the Holy Spirit is said to be that which shows we are owned by God.

BELIEVERS ARE NOW OWNED BY JESUS CHRIST

Paul also wrote to the Corinthians about the seal of Jesus Christ:

> Who also has sealed us and given us the Spirit in our hearts as a guarantee (2 Corinthians 1:21,22 NKJV).

We have been sealed by the Holy Spirit.

To Timothy, Paul emphasized that the Lord knows those people which belong to Him, the true believers. He wrote:

Nevertheless, God's solid foundation stands firm, bearing this inscription: The Lord knows those who are his, and let everyone who calls on the name of the Lord turn away from wickedness (2 Timothy 2:19 CSB).

Thus, those who do belong to Jesus Christ are said to be "sealed." What exactly does this mean?

We find that the impression of a seal implies a relationship to the owner of the seal. It is a means of saying that the thing sealed belongs to the owner.

Believers are God's property with the Holy Spirit being the mark of ownership. In other words, we do not belong to ourselves. Instead we belong to Him.

In the Book of Revelation, we read that God sealed believers with a mark on their foreheads. The Lord said:

> Do not harm the land or the sea or the trees until we put a seal on the foreheads of the servants of our God (Revelation 7:3 NIV).

This is a further illustration that those who belong to Him have His seal or mark.

A CLEAR ILLUSTRATION OF WHAT THIS MEANS

When Paul wrote to the Ephesians that the Holy Spirit was their "seal," the people understood his meaning. In the city of Ephesus, in Paul's day, the following custom was common:

A merchant would go to the harbor and then select certain timber he wanted. He would then seal the timber with his unique impression—an acknowledged sign of ownership. Later the owner would send his servant with his signet. The servant would look for the timber that had the impression of their owner's seal. This is how he would identify the timber that belonged to the merchant.

BELIEVERS HAVE BEEN BOUGHT AT A PRICE

In the same manner God seals those whom He has selected with His sign of ownership—the Holy Spirit. Elsewhere Paul emphasized God's ownership of believers:

> You surely know that your body is a temple where the Holy Spirit lives. The Spirit is in you and is a gift from God. You are no longer your own. God paid a great price for you. So use your body to honor God (1 Corinthians 6:19,20 CEV).

Scripture is clear that He owns us—we belong to Him, not ourselves. The analogy of the sealing of the Holy Spirit emphasizes this essential biblical truth.

SUMMARY TO QUESTION 29
WHY IS THE SEAL, OR INSIGNIA, A SYMBOL OF GOD'S SPIRIT?

The Holy Spirit is compared to a seal or an insignia. The seal is a sign of ownership. God seals those who believe in Jesus Christ with His Holy Spirit. Therefore, when we receive the Holy Spirit this indicates that He now owns us—we do not own ourselves any longer.

When Paul used this analogy of the "seal," it was readily understood by his readers. Ownership of property at that time was indicated by an actual seal or brand which was put on it—such as the branding of timber. Each owner would have his unique brand so there would be no doubt who owned what.

In the same manner, believers in Jesus Christ have our unique "brand" or mark of ownership. It is the Spirit of God who comes into our lives the moment we trust Christ as our Savior. He seals or brands us.

In Scripture, we find it emphasized that we do not belong to ourselves any longer once we trust Christ. We now belong to Jesus Christ because He bought us by means of His death on the cross. Therefore, it should be our desire to serve the One to whom we belong.

Consequently, the analogy of the Holy Spirit "sealing" the believer teaches us a valuable truth.

QUESTION 30

Is There a Difference between the Holy Spirit and the Holy Ghost?

When we read the New Testament, in the *King James* Version of the Bible, we find the Spirit of God variously referred to as the "Holy Spirit" and the "Holy Ghost."

Is there a reason that these two different designations are used? Is it speaking of two different persons, or is it referring to two different aspects of the One Spirit? Why do we find the two different terms?

THERE IS ONLY ONE HOLY SPIRIT

Actually, these verses refer to the One Holy Spirit. There is no theological reason why the Holy Spirit is sometimes referred to as the Holy Ghost. The reason we find the differences has to do with the English language at that time. In Tudor, or Elizabethan English, the word "ghost" simply meant "spirit" at that time in history.

WHY THE DIFFERENCE IN TRANSLATION?

The reason for the difference is found in the story behind the translation of the King James Bible. When the New Testament was translated from Greek into English, it was done by different committees.

One of the committees consistently translated the Greek words *hagion pneuma* as "Holy Spirit" while the other committee translated it as "Holy Ghost." When the translation was completed these differences remained.

Thus, you have the Spirit of God referred to as both the Holy Spirit and the Holy Ghost—yet there is no distinction between the two.

IT HAS BEEN CORRECTED BY MODERN TRANSLATIONS

Modern translations have corrected this inconsistency and have uniformly translated the phrase "hagion pneuma" as Holy Spirit.

The English word "ghost" has taken on a different meaning in our present day. Indeed, it is not always equated with the word "spirit." Therefore, it is not wise to use the term in modern translations because it conjures up a different meaning to the reader.

IT HAS BECOME PART OF CHURCH LANGUAGE

Interestingly, although modern English translations have replaced the outdated term "ghost" with "spirit," some of the liturgy of the church still uses the term.

For example, in the Communion exhortation of the Book of Common Prayer, there is a phrase that reads, "He may receive the benefits of absolution, together with ghostly counsel and advice, to the quieting of his conscience."

Consequently, the word still remains as part of the language of the church though it is hopelessly outdated. We simply do not use the term "ghost" today in the same way.

SUMMARY TO QUESTION 30
IS THERE A DIFFERENCE BETWEEN THE HOLY SPIRIT AND THE HOLY GHOST?

When one reads the Bible in the King James translation they will find that the Third Person of the Trinity is sometimes referred to as the "Holy Spirit," while other times as the "Holy Ghost." We should not assume that it is referring to two different personages.

In Tudor, or Elizabethan, English the words "ghost" and "spirit" meant the same thing. Thus, some ancient translations of Scripture, including the King James Version, have the terms Holy Spirit and Holy Ghost referring to the Spirit of God. Yet there was no difference in meaning at that time.

The reason that both terms were used in the King James translation has to do with the various committees that translated the New Testament. One group consistently used Holy Ghost, while another used Holy Spirit for the same Greek words which referred to the Spirit of God. The inconsistency was not corrected.

Modern versions have corrected this inconsistency with the term "Spirit" replacing the outdated term "ghost." However, some church liturgy still retains this ancient outdated term.

In sum, there is only One Holy Spirit. He is not a "ghost" in the modern sense of the term.

ABOUT THE AUTHOR

Don Stewart is a graduate of Biola University and Talbot Theological Seminary (with the highest honors).

Don is a best-selling and award-winning author having authored, or co-authored, over seventy books. This includes the best-selling *Answers to Tough Questions*, with Josh McDowell, as well as the award-winning book *Family Handbook of Christian Knowledge: The Bible*. His various writings have been translated into over thirty different languages and have sold over a million copies.

Don has traveled around the world proclaiming and defending the historic Christian faith. He has also taught both Hebrew and Greek at the undergraduate level and Greek at the graduate level.

Made in the USA
Las Vegas, NV
21 July 2021